THE
SPECIAL
FORCES
BIBLE

ALEXANDER STILWELL

CHARTWELL
BOOKS, INC.

This edition published in 2013 by
CHARTWELL BOOKS, INC.
A division of BOOK SALES, INC.
276 Fifth Avenue Suite 206
New York, New York 10001
USA

Copyright © 2013 Marshall Editions

Conceived, edited, and designed by
Marshall Editions
The Old Brewery
6 Blundell Street
London N7 9BH
www.marshalleditions.com

Publisher James Ashton-Tyler
Editorial Director Sorrel Wood
Design Paul Turner, Stonecastle Graphics
Copy Editor Charles Phillips
Indexer Diana LeCore
Editorial Assistant Philippa Davis
Production Manager Nikki Ingram

Cover image: MILpictures by Tom Weber/
Getty Images

ISBN-13: 978-0-7858-2985-0

Originated in Hong Kong by Modern Age Repro
House Ltd
Printed and bound in China by Midas Printing
International Limited

Contents

Introduction

Special Operations Forces are highly trained military, naval, or air force personnel who carry out specialized military operations. This book is about their training, skills, equipment, and activities.

READY FOR ANYTHING

Special Forces are different from other elite forces, such as airborne troops or marines, as they are capable of a much wider spectrum of operations and tasks.

WHO DARES WINS

Special Forces were originally conceived as small teams capable of producing a disproportionate effect on the enemy. They use techniques of guerrilla and other forms of unconventional warfare to create surprise and cause disruption. Trained to use a wide range of specialist equipment and weapons, they are highly flexible, use unorthodox methods, and are capable of lateral thinking to solve difficult problems. They can get themselves into and out of trouble using initiative and endurance, and are also capable of making alliances with local forces and winning hearts and minds.

USE COMMON SENSE

The techniques described in this book are used by highly trained military personnel operating under national and international laws of war.

HOW TO USE THIS BOOK

Some of the techniques and training of Special Forces have crossovers with civilian activities, such as climbing or survival techniques. This book provides some useful hints on topics like surviving in an emergency or how to navigate using the stars.

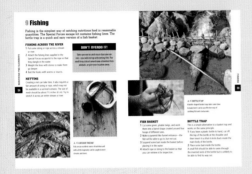

SURVIVAL TECHNIQUES

Special Forces are trained to survive with minimum tools and equipment. This book includes some of the techniques that Special Forces use to survive in the wilderness, including trapping animals for food and making fishing nets, building fires, or building shelters.

INSIGHT INTO TRAINING

To test their physical and mental tenacity, Special Forces recruits are put through the toughest selection and training. This book describes some of the physical and rigorous training they undergo to become the best.

◀ **ESSENTIAL TRAINING**

Special Forces practice a ship assault. Such training is important due to the rise in piracy incidents.

1 ESSENTIAL EQUIPMENT

To maintain agility and speed, Special Forces travel light. Away from regular supply systems, they must carry with them all the equipment they need. In case they have to ditch their rucksack, they carry a specialized belt pouch called an escape kit.

1 What to carry

Special Forces choose their equipment depending on the climate and terrain of each mission. They generally base their equipment on regular issue of the armed forces they serve in, supplemented by additional items bought off the shelf.

CLOTHING LAYERING SYSTEM

- Moisture-wicking base layer
- Shirt
- Fleece or similar
- Waterproof-shell layer
- Gloves
- Boots: Either military issue, or bought off the shelf
- Performance walking socks
- Headwear: Often chosen for warmth and comfort. Special Forces in Afghanistan have been seen wearing local Afghan headwear.

LOOK AFTER YOUR FEET

Soldiers do not take risks when it comes to their feet because they often have to walk a long way. Good boots and performance walking socks are essential.

▼ THE SAME BUT DIFFERENT

Special Forces soldiers from Polish, U.S., and Croatian units, along with a sniper in a ghillie suit.

ESCAPE KIT

When overwhelmed by enemy forces, soldiers are trained to drop their heavy equipment and rely on their escape kit, also called a survival kit:

- Compass
- Heliograph (device for signalling by reflecting sunlight)
- Signal flares
- Flint and steel firelighter
- Windproof matches
- Candle
- Magnifying glass
- Striker board
- Flexible saw
- Swiss Army knife or multi-tool
- Fishing gear—hooks and lines
- Wire snare

▲ **IN CASE OF EMERGENCY**

A marine holds an escape kit—its contents could mean the difference between life and death in an emergency.

- Needles and safety pins
- Razor
- Whistle
- Water bag
- Water purification tablets
- Antiseptic
- Plasters
- Potassium permanganate—used as a disinfectant and to purify water.

2 SURVIVING THE ELEMENTS

Special Forces soldiers follow an intensive training program in arctic survival, jungle survival, and urban warfare. Outdoor survival skills are crucial—it is likely soldiers will have to evade an enemy or escape capture in open country where there is no form of supply or support.

2 Escape and survive

Special Forces are taught how to get out of an area on foot as part of survival training. After the escape, you are faced with two major challenges: Evading the enemy and surviving in the wild.

GET SAFE, BE READY

The first priority is to make sure you are in a safe place and ready to repel any attack.

SURVIVAL

Survival in the wild requires ingenuity, endurance, and good basic training.

S—Size up your surroundings

- Observe enemy movements and locations.
- Check how close you are to urban areas or roads. What are the dangers of being spotted by civilians?
- Assess the best places to find shelter and hide.
- Look out for sources of food and water.
- Assess your own physical condition. Do you have wounds that need attention?
- What equipment do you have? Do you have an escape kit?

U—Use all senses

- You need to be as alert as an animal in the wild.
- After the trauma of an escape or other incident you need to take time to calm your thoughts.
- Fight the impulse to panic or take immediate action. Don't do anything ill-considered.
- You may need to remain in your safe place until dusk—especially if there are enemy troops around or civilians who might report you.

- Plan what you will do if you are seen.
- Take advantage of the noise of a passing aircraft or vehicle to move into a better position without being heard.

R—Remember your location

- You need to work out your location—either with a map and compass, if you have them, or by observing your surroundings.
- Identify enemy positions and areas where local civilians may be unfriendly.
- Work out a route to get you back to safety.

V—Vanquish fear and panic

- Calming yourself down may be the key to survival.
- Dehydration and hunger can make it difficult to think clearly, so—after checking that you are safe from enemy observation—make a plan to get hold of the essentials you need for survival.

I—Improvise

- If you still have your escape kit, you'll have access to several essential tools to help you survive. Your most immediate need will probably be for a knife to cut branches to build a shelter.
- Otherwise, you'll need to make best use of the natural materials around you to make yourself as safe, warm, and as comfortable as possible.

▲ MAINTAINING MOMENTUM
Confidence, strength, and teamwork are an essential part of Special Forces training.

V—Value living

Special Forces training places high value on endurance. In training you will often have been deprived of sleep and forced to keep going. This kind of training is a real benefit in a survival situation—you may need to build a shelter and forage for food and water despite being cold, wet, and exhausted.

- Remember your training.
- Feed on your determination to survive. This will keep you going.

A—Act like the natives

- Depending on what country you are in, you may find allies among the native people.
- If locals are friendly, they may provide food, water, and shelter but be wary of the possibility of informers. Special Forces units in the past have been compromised by seemingly friendly wandering shepherds.
- By observing animal life around you, look out for clues as to where to find water.
- Be wary of disturbing animals and birds in case their sudden movements give away your presence to enemy patrols or civilians.

L—Live by your wits and use your basic skills

- Remember that your intensive survival training tested you when you were deprived of food and water. You have proved you have the strength and will to endure.
- No matter how exhausted and weak you may feel, make sure you attend to the basics of survival.

3 Emergency first aid

Swift action in a medical emergency can be the difference between life and death. One out of four soldiers in a Special Forces team will have advanced medical training.

EMERGENCY CHECK, ABC

The first questions soldiers will ask in an emergency are:

- Is it safe?
- Is the casualty still in a dangerous situation?

The next sequence of actions can be easily memorized with the acronym **ABC**.

▼ ADVANCE TRAINING

Special Forces are trained in first aid skills to enable quick reactions and decisions in a real emergency.

SIMPLE AS ABC

A—AIRWAY

Open the mouth of the casualty and check that there is nothing blocking the throat or interfering with breathing.

B—BREATHING

Place your cheek near to the casualty's nose and mouth and listen and feel for signs of breathing (see below, left).

C—CIRCULATION

To check for a pulse, place your fingers on the underside of the wrist on the inside of the wrist tendon (see below). Alternatively, feel for a pulse on the neck on the side of the windpipe.

APPLYING A FIELD DRESSING

Special Forces soldiers are usually issued with a field dressing that can be applied to a wound to stem blood flow.

1 Remove clothing from around the wound, cutting it away if necessary. Carefully wash the skin around the wound with clean water and irrigate the wound to remove any dirt.

2 Open the wrapper to reveal the dressing, taking care not to touch the white underside of the dressing.

▼ **ACT QUICK TO SAVE LIVES**
Quick action such as applying a field dressing can help to stabilize a casualty's condition before they reach a field hospital.

3 Place the dressing directly onto the wound. Wrap the bandage tails attached to the dressing around the body or limb in opposite directions, bringing them back over the dressing to keep it firmly in place and around the sides of the dressing to seal off the wound area and prevent dirt getting in.

4 Tie a square knot (also known as a reef knot, see page 26) in the two tail ends to keep the dressing in place.

5 Ensure the bandage is tight enough to keep the dressing secure and to stem blood flow, but not so tight as to cause circulation problems.

6 If the wound is in a limb, raise the limb slightly above the level of the heart and support it there.

4 Building a shelter

Special Forces troops often have to set up covert shelters or hides so they can observe enemy movements and call in artillery or aerial fire.

LEAN-TO SHELTER

1 Place a horizontal pole between two trees—or between one tree and an upright pole you have placed there yourself. You can create a firm base by binding lengths of wood in a rectangular arrangement.

2 Lean poles against the horizontal pole (on the windy side of the shelter) and bind them together.

3 Place further upright poles on each side to form the basis of the walls.

4 Lean leafy branches against the frame to provide protection.

DESERT SHELTER

1 Find a sunken area of ground or dig a shallow trench about 2 feet (60 cm) deep.

2 Place a poncho liner over the area and anchor it with stones or sand.

3 Place a second poncho over the first, leaving a gap of about 18 inches (45 cm). This creates an insulating layer to keep the area within cool.

▼ **BASIC SHELTER**

The lean-to shelter is one of the simplest and most effective temporary shelters and can be easily constructed.

5 Finding water

Water is a top priority. If it is not readily available from streams or rivers, there are several methods for capturing water.

GETTING WATER IN ARID AREAS

- Look in the lowest point or outside bend of a dried water course—water will collect here.
- Follow animals—they will often be heading toward water.
- Look in holes in rocks or in caves, where water may have collected.
- You can wring water out of a cloth containing wet mud.
- Heat snow and ice to obtain water.

▶ **THIRSTY?**
A Special Forces soldier can survive without many things but not without water. Plants can provide essential liquid.

DO IT YOURSELF SOLAR STILL

How to capture dew for drinking water:

1 Dig a round hole approximately 3 feet (1 m) across and 2 feet (60 cm) deep.

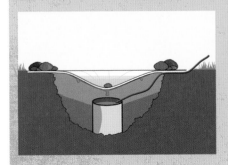

2 Place a container at the bottom of the hole.

3 Place one end of a tube in the container and pass the other end to the edge of the hole (to drink from).

4 Place a plastic sheet over the hole and secure it leaving the end of the tube free.

5 Place a small stone in the center of the sheet so that it causes the sheet to dip.

6 Dew drips into the container. Using the tube, drink the water that collects.

6 Building fires

When you build a fire, choose a sheltered area and make sure it has a firm base. Some types of fire are better for warmth and some better for cooking.

THEY ALL BURN

Depending on what's available, you can use any of several elements to build a fire, including:

- Wood shavings
- Pine needles or bird down
- Logs, bark, or paper
- Dead branches
- Dry animal dung, or dry grasses twisted together

BE PREPARED!

Fire-lighting equipment in the emergency survival kit includes windproof matches, a magnifying glass, or a flint and steel.

FIRESTARTER

In sunny conditions, a magnifying glass can be used to pinpoint the sun's rays to start a fire in dry kindling.

FLAMING TEPEE

A tepee fire is good for both warmth and cooking.

1 Poke a stick into the ground at a slant.
2 Lean other sticks against the slanted stick.
3 Light the fire, keeping your back to the wind.

STAR BRIGHT

A star fire is best made with hardwood logs.

1 Arrange the logs in a star shape.
2 As the ends at the center burn away, gradually push each log further in.

▼ KEEP WARM

As long as the tactical situation allows it, a fire can provide both physical warmth as well as hot food and drink.

20

7 Finding food

Special Forces are trained to distinguish between edible and poisonous plants. If in doubt, carry out an edibility test.

CAN I EAT THIS?

- **Inspect** Look for obvious signs of decay.
- **Smell** Avoid if bitter.
- **Test for skin irritation** If it irritates the skin, discard it.
- **Try** Place a small portion of the plant on the corner of your mouth, the tip of your tongue, and under your tongue. If there is no reaction, chew a small part.
- **Swallow test** Swallow a small amount and wait about five hours. If all is fine, you can use the plant for food.

Edible plants include crab apple (raw or boiled) and nettles, which can be boiled to make a nutritious and healthy tea.

◄▲ SUPERFOODS IN THE WILD

Wild fruits such as blueberries (above) or durian fruit (left), are an excellent source of nutrition. Tropical areas are particularly rich in fruits which can help a soldier to survive for long periods in the bush.

ALWAYS AVOID

- Overripe fruit or anything with mildew or fungus
- Anything that has a smell of almonds— this indicates cyanide
- Mushrooms—unless you know they are safe
- Plants with a three-leaf pattern
- Grain heads with pink, purple, or black spurs
- Foliage looking like carrot, parsnip, parsley, or dill

8 Tracking and trapping animals

There are several methods of catching animals for food, some of which involve using exotic traps. The standard escape kit includes nonferrous metal snares, for catching small animals such as rabbits, and lines for catching fish.

TRACKING ANIMALS

Look for the following signs of animal tracks:

- Spoor
- Flattened undergrowth
- Broken spiders' webs
- Passages cleared in dew
- Gnawed twigs or tree trunks

SIMPLE SNARE TRAP

A snare is best set on the known path of an animal and in a place where the animals have to run through it—for example, a natural tunnel.

1 To set a metal snare, anchor one end securely to a stake or to another firm base and position the open hoop so that an animal's head is likely to pass through it, i.e. raising it off the ground with a couple of twigs.

2 Once the snare is set, disguise the ground around it by spreading leaves and foliage.

TOOLS AND WEAPONS

If necessary, Special Forces soldiers will make their own bow and arrow or slingshot to aid hunting.

BOW AND ARROW

1 Select a supple sapling.

2 Whittle the stave to about 2 inches (5 cm) wide at the center and about $5/8$ inch (1.5 cm) at either end.

3 Cut notches at the ends and attach string.

4 Cut arrows to about 2 feet (60 cm) long and about $1/4$ inch (6 mm) wide.

5 Cut a notch in the end of each arrow.

6 Split bird-feather quills down the middle, and bind three half-quills of feathers in an even spacing around the arrow shaft.

7 The arrowhead can be sharp flint, tin, or bone. Alternatively, whittle wood to a point and then heat it over a fire.

SLINGSHOT

Take a leather thong, rope, string, or similar material and sew a pouch in the center. Use a stone as a missile.

To throw with a slingshot, swing it above your head and then release one of the strings when your arm is pointing at the target.

MAKING ARROWS
A soldier carefully binds a turkey
feather to an arrow shaft. Natural
resources such as these make
effective weapons for hunting.

9 Fishing

Fishing is the simplest way of catching nutritious food in reasonable quantities. The Special Forces escape kit contains fishing lines. The bottle trap is a quick and easy version of a fish basket.

FISHING ACROSS THE RIVER

1 Put some string or rope across a stream or river.

2 Attach the fishing lines supplied in the Special Forces escape kit to the rope so that they dangle in the water.

3 Weight the lines with stones to make them go deeper.

4 Bait the hooks with worms or insects.

NETTING

Creating a net can take time. It also requires a fair amount of string or rope, which may not be available in a survival scenario. The size of mesh should be about 1½ inches (4 cm). Try to stretch it across an entire stream or river.

DON'T OVERDO IT!

Take care not to catch more than you can eat—you will end up with rotting fish. The smell may attract unwelcome attention from animals, or give your location away.

▲◀ CATCH OF THE DAY
Fish are an excellent source of nutrition and with a little ingenuity can be caught in most streams and rivers.

▲◀ BOTTLE IT UP
A bottle-shaped basket trap takes some time
to make but it can be an effective way of
catching fish and crustaceans.

FISH BASKET

1 Cut some green, pliable twigs, and work
  them into a barrel shape created around four
  hoops of different sizes.
2 Make a pyramid-like funnel entrance—the
  fish will be able to go in, but not out.
3 Suspend some bait inside the basket before
  placing it in the water.
4 Attach rope or string to the basket so that
  you can retrieve it for inspection.

BOTTLE TRAP

This is a simple alternative to a basket trap and
works on the same principle.
1 If you have a plastic bottle to hand, cut off
  the top of the bottle at the shoulder and
  then invert it so that it sticks back inside the
  main body of the bottle.
2 Place some bait inside the bottle.
A small fish should be able to swim through
the inverted neck of the bottle but is unlikely to
be able to find its way out.

10 Ropes and knots

The U.S. Navy SEALs (Sea, Air, Land) learn five essential knots as part of their basic training. Recruits are expected to be able tie these knots underwater.

1 SQUARE KNOT

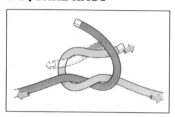

Also known as a reef knot, this is useful for joining two pieces of rope or string, but it is not 100-percent secure.

1 Place the right working end over the left working end.
2 Pull the right end back and over the top of the left rope.
3 Place the left working end over the right working end and pull it under and back over the left rope.

2 BOWLINE

The bowline is used for creating a loop at the end of a rope. It can be easily tied and untied.

1 Create a small loop by passing the working end over the standing part.
2 Bring the end back toward the loop.
3 Pass the working end through the back of the loop, then turn it behind the standing part.
4 Bring the working end back to the front of the loop and pass the end through the front.
5 Tighten the knot, leaving a loop large enough to work with.

3 SHEET BEND

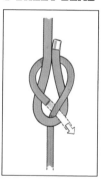

A sheet bend—or becket bend—is used to join two lines together.

1 Create a bight in one of the working ends of the two lines and then pass the working end of the other line through it.
2 Take the working end round behind the bight and then pass it through the standing part of the second line.
3 Then work the knot so that it is tight.

4 CLOVE HITCH AND
5 RIGHT-ANGLE KNOT

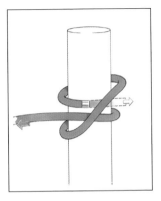

The clove hitch is used to attach a rope to a post or a climbing rope to a carabiner.

1 Take the working end around the object you want to attach the rope to, make a turn and cross the working end over the standing part.
2 Bring the working end around again toward the crossover.
3 Pass the tip of the working end through the loop on the crossover.
4 Work the hitch so that it is tight.

The right angle knot can be used as an alternative to a clove hitch. It is often used to attach an explosive detonation cord, tie a rope to a post, or as a temporary attachment to an anchor point.

To tie a right-angle knot: Make two turns around the object at step one (instead of a single turn).

OVERHAND KNOT

A permanent knot, can be used to prevent ends unravelling (see page 148).

▶ **UP AND OVER**
A strong rope, a carabiner, and a correctly-tied knot enable a soldier to traverse a river or other obstacles.

ESCAPE TACTICS

As a Special Forces operative you are trained in escape strategies in case you are captured.

GET AWAY EARLY

There are major benefits from making an early escape if you are captured. Your enemy may be tired and hungry after an engagement, and your captors may not have enough troops to both guard the remaining prisoners and go after you. The enemy may be unfamiliar with the area and find it difficult to track you if you get away.

QUICK WITS

You'll need to be quick-witted to identify a chance to sneak away from your captors. Look for opportunities. Watch for moments when your captors may be distracted.

COVER YOUR TRACKS

If you manage to escape after being captured, use Special Forces countertracking

ON THE RUN?

Don't use scented soap or wear aftershave—or even polish your boots—when on the run in open country. Even without the aid of a dog, an experienced enemy may be able to detect your presence just from his or her sense of smell.

techniques—see pages 37-41. Your immediate priority is to get as far from your captors as possible, as quickly as you can.

▼ NATURE'S AFTERSHAVE
Soldiers crawl through mud to disguise their scent during an escape and evasion exercise.

11 Break out from the enemy base

Once you have been taken to the enemy base, you'll be guarded more carefully and placed in a restricted area. Closely monitor the movements of camp guards and study general routines. Plot carefully when to make your move.

▲ UNDER THE WIRE
A soldier demonstrates speed, agility, and determination as he passes under a barbed-wire obstacle.

CONFUSE YOUR GUARDS

If you have been captured with fellow-operatives, work together. This is a well-tried scheme:
1 Your fellow-prisoner feigns an injury and collapses, refusing to go further.
2 While the guards are distracted, seize the opportunity to make a break for it.

BE PREPARED

When you embark on a mission where you may be captured, plan group escape strategies in advance, just in case. Once you have been captured, you might not get a chance to discuss ways to break away. Plans involving two or more Special Forces operatives are most likely to work (see panel left).

BEATING BARBED WIRE

You'll need a blanket to counter barbed wire fences. Place the blanket over the top of the fence and then roll over it.

3 TRACKING

Know your enemy—Special Forces learn tracking from both perspectives: As the pursuer, to hunt down terrorists, and as evaders, escaping from capture or returning from a mission behind enemy lines. This chapter includes essential skills used by trackers to determine where and when their quarry passed and also the tricks of the trade for how to evade a dog-tracker team.

12 Understanding the lay of the land

When tracking study the landscape carefully and look out for common-sense clues as to where your quarry may be or what route they are most likely to have taken. Bear in mind that they may have deliberately chosen a less obvious route in order to avoid detection.

THE WELL-CONCEALED ROUTE

Think about which route you would be most likely to take if you wished to remain concealed—for example along a hedgerow or behind a stone wall.

NATURE'S WATCH DOGS

If you think your quarry may be in the area, look out for any clues from animal or bird behavior. Birds may suddenly fly up from long grass if someone is there or they may start to avoid a particular area.

▼ PATHFINDING
Careful observation of the terrain will reveal whether someone has passed through the area recently.

13 Working with the weather and vegetation

RAINING CLUES

Weather conditions can radically affect your ability to track and find your quarry. A fresh fall of snow, for example, may conceal evidence underneath it but it may also mean you can see footprints clearly. Driving rain may wash away valuable evidence but drops of rain in a footprint leave a clue to when your quarry passed through.

VEGETATION CLUES

IN AN AREA WITH LEAVES AND TWIGS
Slight depressions, upturned or crumpled leaves, and bent and broken twigs.

IN A GRASSY AREA
Tall grass brushed in one direction or a shadow in shorter grass, either because the grass is bent or dew has been disturbed.

NEAR WATER
Where water, mud, or sand has been splashed or carried onto nearby vegetation.

GRASS CLASS

Vegetation can provide a host of important clues. First, examine the vegetation in an area to see what the normal state is then look around for signs that anything has changed.

▲ WHO, WHERE, WHEN?
An experienced tracker will not only be able to detect the route taken by a unit but also how many troops there were in the unit.

14 Tracking animals

Special Forces may need to track animals for food if they are in a survival situation. Identifying the animal track, such as a rabbit or deer, is therefore useful. Experienced trackers will be able to detect how recently the animal has passed through the area and will also be able to plan how to trap an animal for food.

An experienced tracker will soon be aware of what kind of animal they are dealing with not only because of the imprint but how it falls. A walking cat, for example, places its back paw in exactly the same place as the front paw and the tracks are arranged in a straight line.

WALKING PATTERNS

A horse moves its legs in a diagonal way (front right followed by back left and so on). However, the pattern changes when the horse moves into a trot and then a gallop. A rabbit or a kangaroo throws itself forward, with its hind legs landing in front of its fore legs.

ANIMAL IDENTIFIERS

- The way that they use their feet
- Shape of the imprint
- Length of their legs
- The way they move at different speeds

ANIMAL PRINTS

- Walking **on the soles** of their feet: Humans, gorillas, bears, and rabbits
- Walking **on their toes**: Dogs and cats
- Walking **on tip-toes**, the nails hardening into hooves which are either solid: Horses and zebras; or cloven: Deer, moose, and sheep

▶ FOOD OR FOE?
Identifying animal tracks can be useful, either to evade dangerous animals or to track animals for food.

15 Reading human tracks

When following human quarry, the tracker will look for identifying marks that help him to check he is following the same person.

BAREFOOT

- Length of toes
- Spread of toes
- Instep (flat foot or raised arch)
- Size of ball of foot and metatarsals
- Other distinguishing marks

SHOE OR BOOT

- Tread pattern
- Logo
- Signs of wear
- Other identifying marks such as arrangement of shoe tacks or stone lodged in the tread

The tracker will also be looking out for evidence of the way the quarry moves. When walking, humans tend to splay their feet to left and right for better balance. When jogging, the foot fall becomes more centralized as balance is less of an issue (due to increased forward momentum). When running, the footfall may be concentrated on the front of the foot, showing just a toe imprint rather than a full foot imprint.

▶ **HIDDEN DETAIL**

Although these footprints are obvious, an experienced tracker will be able to deduce less obvious information such as speed of travel.

PACKING?

The tracker can also trace whether the person is carrying a load (splayed feet and pronounced imprint) or limping (deeper impression from one foot).

THE "LOST TRACK" DRILL

Sometimes the track disappears. This may be due to the ground becoming harder or the quarry may have clambered over some rocks.

1 Mark the place of the last known track. Place a stick or stone next to it.

2 Make an initial search around a half circle in front of you. Do this standing, then kneeling, then from ground level. An imprint that is invisible from above may be visible when viewed from the side or at ground level.

3 If there is still no sign, move outward from the point of the last sign to a distance of about five yards (5 m) at 90 degrees to the left of the line of march, then at 45 degrees, then straight forward and so on until reaching 90 degrees to the right of the line of march.

▼ **PLAN YOUR SEARCH**
A coordinated search is most likely to find a lost track.

If there is still no sign of a track, use one of the following three methods.

BOX METHOD

Move forward from the point of the last identifiable track for about 200 yards (200 m). Then turn right and walk about 100 yards (100 m). Return to the line of the last track and turn left to return to the start point. Then repeat the whole process again—this time to the left of the original track.

360-DEGREE SEARCH METHOD

Make a series of ever-widening circles around the point of the last identifiable track. The advantage of this search method is that you can search all the way around the last track and not just to the front of it.

CROSS-GRAIN METHOD

Having checked the ground in front of the last identifiable track, search to the right for about 100 yards (100 m), then to the left, parallel to the original line of march, for about 50 yards (50 m), then left again to cross the forward line of march and beyond for approximately 100 yards (100 m), then right, forward about 50 yards (50 m) and so on, criss-crossing the forward line of march and steadily covering the ground.

16 Countertracking

A tracker may come across a range of deception tactics used by the quarry. These may include walking backward, walking on tip-toe, sweeping away footprints, walking on stones and boulders, walking through streams, and looping back.

Experienced trackers may be able to detect most of these for the following reasons:

- When walking backward, the body weight is thrown onto the heel of the shoe and this makes a recognizably different imprint to one where someone is walking forward.
- Walking on tip-toes is easily detected and is uncomfortable for the quarry to maintain for any length of time.
- It is often obvious where an area has been swept. Look around the edges of the swept area to continue following the trail.
- Experienced trackers can detect signs of movement even on boulders, due to small deposits or displacement of dust.
- Walking through streams often leaves obvious clues: Stones and pebbles at the bottom of the stream will be displaced and show a different color where mud or silt has been moved.
- The exit point from the stream or river is usually clear from imprints on the ground and disturbed vegetation. If the quarry leaves the water backward, the tracker may detect this due to the obvious imprint type mentioned above.
- Looping back can be a threat to the tracker as the quarry may be lying in wait for him and you should therefore be even more cautious of walking into an ambush.

▲ **UNCOVER DECEPTION**
Wading though water can confuse a pursuer but skilled trackers can often detect disturbance in a river bed.

17 Double tracking

This is a more sophisticated and potentially more effective way of losing or delaying a tracker.

ZIGZAG METHOD

1 Walk toward a tree in a clearing for about five paces.
2 Turn around and walk backward, changing direction by 40 degrees.
3 Repeat this maneuver at another location further on.

▼ CONFUSE TO LOSE
There are various methods of confusing a pursuer in order to buy time and have a better chance of escape.

CROSS-TRAIL METHOD

1 Approach a trail at an angle of 45 degrees.
2 Move along the trail for about 66–98 feet (20–30 m), leaving obvious footprints.
3 Walk backward along the trail to the point where you first joined it.
4 Carefully cross the trail to the other side, taking care not to leave signs that you have done so.

18 How to evade tracker dogs

A dog with an experienced handler is a formidable opponent. Once a dog has been given the scent of a piece of clothing or anything used by the evader, it will be able to follow the scent either on the ground or in the air in either a rural or an urban environment.

WHY TRACKER DOGS ARE YOUR ENEMY

THEY CAN SMELL PARTICLES OF SKIN
A dog's sense of smell is about 900 times more efficient than a human's. Not only can a dog pick up obvious scents like body odor or deodorant, it can also detect the odor of microscopic particles of hair or skin invisible to the human eye.

WHAT BIG EARS YOU HAVE ...
A dog's hearing is about 40 times more efficient than human hearing. With their large ears, they can pick up sounds effectively and also accurately target the direction of the sound. They can also filter peripheral sounds in order to focus on the relevant ones.

FREEZE!
Dog eyesight is not particularly remarkable but they can detect movement more efficiently than humans.

OUT RUNNED AND OUT GUNNED
A dog can reach speeds of up to 40 mph (64 km/h). However, this can only be sustained over relatively short distances. When tracking a dog's speed is also limited by the speed of the handler.

19 Evading dogs

If you have a dog on your trail, you are in trouble. Your best chance is to wear down the dog and handler team.

DOGGONE EVASION TECHNIQUES

- Double back and go around clumps of vegetation—this may delay the dog and even tangle the lead.
- Move with the wind behind your back so there is less body scent.
- Pass through herds of livestock in a rural area or crowds in an urban setting.
- Use a bicycle or car to minimize the scent trail.
- Climb a high fence that will be difficult for the dog and handler to climb.
- Using water obstacles may delay a dog but if the dog gets to the other side of the water it may be able to pick up the scent where you left the water.

DON'T POP THE PEPPER

Using a distracting agent such as pepper particles will not make much difference. The dog will just sneeze and have a clearer nose to keep on your track!

▼ TRAINED TO TRACK AND ATTACK
Dogs have exceptional tracking skills and are very difficult to evade but you can try to confuse the dog and tracker team.

WHICH TRACKER DOG?

GERMAN SHEPHERD/ ALSATIAN

The German shepherd is an excellent tracker and attack dog. It is intelligent, eager to learn, and has a strong bite. These dogs bond well with their owners and are highly obedient.

DOBERMAN PINSCHER

Originally bred as an aggressive guard dog, the Doberman is very loyal to its owners and highly intelligent. Due to their strength and aggression Dobermans make formidable tracker and attack dogs.

▶ GERMAN SHEPHERD
▼ BLOODHOUND

LABRADOR

A popular, social dog the Labrador does not have the aggressive reputation of the two breeds above. Highly intelligent, with good initiative and an excellent sense of smell, they are best used for tracking rather than aggressive roles. Labradors are employed by both the U.S. and British armed forces.

BLOODHOUND

A famous breed of tracker dog with a long history of tracking humans. The bloodhound has larger nasal chambers than most other dogs. The drooping ears help to trap scents and prevent interference from the wind. The bloodhound is not aggressive but is very determined when on the scent.

4
COMMUNICATIONS

Highly mobile, Special Forces require sophisticated communications to keep pace with them. They use high-level communications to report enemy movements, identify targets for interception, coordinate precisely planned assault operations, and follow high-value suspects.

20 High-tech surveillance

For a target-observation mission Special Forces move covertly to a designated area and set up surveillance equipment—this may range from simple binoculars to infrared sighting equipment.

GETTING IN POSITION

During a mission, the Special Forces unit is expected to move into the operational area unobserved, communicate covertly for the allotted time period, and then extract back to base without getting caught. Patrols can be infiltrated into position by water or land through:

- "Stay behind" tactics—the operational area is set up prior to friendly forces pulling back behind their position
- Aircraft or parachute landing

SATELLITE COMMUNICATIONS

A special operations unit may carry a light, portable satellite antenna for communication via satellite to homeland headquarters or to other unit bases in different parts of the world.

Designers are working to make these systems lighter and more portable. They are developing systems that work with commercially available lithium batteries, and introducing higher-gain antennae on satellites, so that the portable antennae do not have to be so powerful.

STAYING INCOGNITO

Concealing your identity during a mission is essential. Signaling equipment often includes fast-burst technology, which makes it more difficult for enemy signal detection equipment to pinpoint the source of the signal.

INTELLIGENT RADIO

A typical team will be equipped with a handheld multi-band tactical software-defined radio. A software-defined radio has several advantages over a standard radio system—it can intelligently lock on to the best frequencies and work cooperatively with other radios in the net.

▶ KEEP IN TOUCH
Carrying lightweight portable satellite equipment allows Special Forces to communicate with other teams and headquarters worldwide.

21 Key information on the enemy

Special Forces units are often tasked with providing detailed information on enemy movements and other activities.

SALUTE

The acronym SALUTE summarizes important intelligence-gathering:

S—Size Identify number of enemy personnel, number of vehicles, or overall size of units.

A—Activity Establish whether enemy personnel are engaged in offensive movements, infiltrating a given area, taking in supplies, and so on.

L—Location Provide the best possible coordinates for enemy positions, giving map references or through laser-assisted designation of the target area.

U—Unit Identify specific units through badges on vehicles, type of vehicles, type of uniform, and so on.

T—Time Provide real time or adjusted time if the observation is in a different time zone from the base to which they are reporting.

E—Equipment Report on number and type of vehicles, artillery, small arms, and communications equipment.

▼ ACCESS ALL AREAS
Advanced tactical radio communications enable soldiers to coordinate effectively with both air and ground forces.

22 Forward air controlling

Precision weapons make it possible to hit specific targets with less risk of collateral damage. Close Air Support (CAS) is accompanied by a Ground-Aided Precision Strike (GAPS).

COMMUNICATIONS

ID THE ENEMY

Special Forces on the ground have to provide positive identification of:
- The target
- Location of enemy forces

To improve accuracy and communication, teams detailed to designate targets for aerial assets have an air force combat controller as part of the team.

MINIMIZING COLLATERAL DAMAGE

- Ideally the aircraft pilot and navigator have sight of friendly locations—this is best provided through a moving map in the attack aircraft.
- Special Forces carry a beacon that can be identified by the aircraft.
- Beyond line-of-sight reporting and tasking system (BRAT) can be deployed to identify friendly forces. This can be scaled down to identify individual friendly soldiers in the battlefield.

PAINTING THE TARGET

Special Forces in Iraq and Afghanistan use a Special Operations Forces Laser Acquisition Marker (SOFLAM).

LASERS

A laser beam is fired at the target, creating a reflection that is detected by an aircraft or intelligent missile. This is known as "painting the target." The equipment can also be used for range-finding by artillery spotters.

LIGHTWEIGHT

The most highly developed version of SOFLAM carries a single, lightweight battery and is more compact overall than previous versions.

The system is relatively easy to carry as it weighs just 17.3 lbs (5.2 kg) and has a volume of only 435 cubic inches (7,100 cubic cm). It can mark targets more than 6 miles (10 km) away.

◀ **LOCATING THE ENEMY**
Using sophisticated target-acquisition
equipment, Special Forces can bring in
devastating aerial attacks against an enemy.

▲ **POISED TO ATTACK**
Airfields and other sensitive areas can be
protected by automated missile systems
such as Rapier.

LASER DESIGNATORS

In the stress of battle even Special Forces can
make mistakes if equipment is unwieldy—and
there may be "fat finger" issues, when people
make errors while tapping out coordinates.

Modular Advance Reconnaissance System
(MARS) brings together Leica Geosystems
Viper laser rangefinder binoculars, used for
triangulating targets, and a Global Positioning
System (GPS) PLGR system that can convert a
laser spot to latitude and longitude.

This increasingly automated system
provides target accuracy to 13 feet (4 m).
Coordinates are transmitted to the aircraft by
voice radio.

23 Encryption

Encryption involves disguising information so that it can only be interpreted and understood by someone who has the key to decrypt the message.

FAST-BURST TRANSMISSIONS

Special Forces use advanced radios capable of communicating encrypted digital data in tandem with fast-burst technology. This enables them to send encrypted data in a very short space of time, minimizing the chance of enemy signal-detection equipment providing a direction to the source of the transmission.

ONE-TIME PAD

In the British Army, Special Forces carry a one-time pad, part of the British Army BATCO system of cryptography. This system involves a pad and a pencil. It remains secure so long as only the user and the receiver have access to the relevant issue of the pad.

Soldiers are trained to destroy their one-time pads as a priority if they are in danger of capture by the enemy.

▼ SCRAMBLE KEY INTELLIGENCE
Encryption devices, such as this CYZ-10 device, make it very hard for an enemy to intercept or interpret messages.

COMMUNICATIONS

48

MORSE CODE

The Morse code has been overtaken by satellite technology, and is not widely used for communication, but it can still be a useful fallback if more sophisticated equipment fails.

Letter	Morse code	Verbal signal
A	. —	Alpha
B	— . . .	Bravo
C	— . — .	Charlie
D	— . .	Delta
E	.	Echo
F	. . — .	Foxtrot
G	— — .	Golf
H	. . . .	Hotel
I	. .	India
J	. — — —	Juliet
K	— . —	Kilo
L	. — . .	Lima
M	— —	Mike
N	— .	November
O	— — —	Oscar
P	. — — .	Papa
Q	— — . —	Quebec
R	. — .	Romeo
S	. . .	Sierra
T	—	Tango
U	. . —	Uniform
V	. . . —	Victor
W	. — —	Whiskey
X	— . . —	X-ray
Y	— . — —	Yankee
Z	— — . .	Zulu

Number	Morse code	Verbal signal
1	. — — — —	One
2	. . — — —	Two
3	. . . — —	Three
4	. . . . —	Four
5	. . . . .	Five
6	—	Six
7	— — . . .	Seven
8	— — — . .	Eight
9	— — — — .	Nine
0	— — — — —	Zero

▲ NATO CODE

The NATO phonetic alphabet provides standard code words for each letter of the alphabet. These verbal signifiers are used worldwide to make sure orders are properly relayed.

▶ FLASH COMMUNICATION

Morse code flashes signals between ships.

5 SPECIAL RECONNAISSANCE

Special Forces armed soldiers are distinct from the security agencies such as the CIA and FBI. However, missions do involve a large measure of surveillance and there is a gray area between Special Forces' work and espionage.

24 Reconnaissance 101

Special Forces are sent on a variety of reconnaissance missions.

AREA ASSESSMENT

Collecting and evaluating information about a country, region, or other area.

GEOGRAPHICAL RECONNAISSANCE

Gathering information about a specific locale in advance of a planned operation. For example, units such as U.S. Navy SEALs or British Special Boat Service provide information in advance of a landing on a beach, including:

- Whether the beach is suitable for a landing
- Where enemy defenses are sited and how many there are
- Enemy movements

SIGNALS AND TECHNICAL INTELLIGENCE

This kind of mission may involve:

- Direction-finding of enemy signals, including location of signals centers and headquarters
- Capture of enemy equipment and information for analysis.

▼ COVERT APPROACH
Special Forces can emerge from the sea to carry out reconnaissance or to attack an enemy position.

ACCESS ALL SECTORS

Due to the importance of Special Forces reconnaissance feedback is often dealt with at the highest military and political levels. Surveillance operations may be feeding information to a variety of sectors at any one time:

HUMAN INTELLIGENCE (HUMINT)

Intelligence gathered through human contact. This includes information gathered from captured enemy personnel or from friendly civilians.

IMAGERY INTELLIGENCE (IMINT)

Operations may involve visual surveillance of insurgent leaders in an urban environment.

SIGNALS INTELLIGENCE (SIGINT)

Includes direction-finding to locate enemy signaling positions and headquarters, tapping into enemy signals networks to gather information, and disrupting enemy signals through offensive electronic warfare. A specialist signals unit may be involved in such missions.

TARGET ACQUISITION

Special Forces SR (special reconnaissance) units may be tasked with finding specific targets, such as the Scud launchers during Operation Desert Storm in Iraq.

In a Ground-Aided Precision Strike (GAPS) a target is "painted" with laser-guidance systems so that aerial fighters or bombers can attack the target with precision guided weapons (see page 46).

▶ SPYING FROM A DISTANCE
Systems such as the Long Range Advanced Scout Surveillance System (LRAS3) allow Special Forces to track enemy movements over long distances.

25 Covert surveillance

The key to a successful covert surveillance mission lies in selecting and setting up a good fixed observation post—or more, if necessary.

KEY FACTORS FOR A GOOD OBSERVATION POST
1 FIELD OF VIEW

A mission may require more than one observation post. This may be for security reasons—for example, one point for day and one for night, or because no one site provides a sufficient field of vision on its own.

▼ SCOUTING OUT THE ENEMY
Covert surveillance can provide key information on enemy movements for commanders.

2 SECURITY

How likely is it to be seen by the enemy? Question if it is an area that could be compromised by enemy patrols, or by civilians, such as shepherds grazing their sheep or goats.

3 CONSTRUCTION OF THE SITE

Is it a reasonably habitable place for the observers? Members of the surveillance team must be able to communicate easily with base, store their equipment, and eat and sleep comfortably for what may be a considerable period of time.

COVERT SURVEILLANCE

◀ **EYES EVERYWHERE**
High-tech devices such as miniature cameras can be easily concealed on the ground and contribute to the overall intelligence picture.

SITE GOT THE BLUES?

U.S. and other Special Forces use the mnemonic BLUES to assess the suitability of a site.

B—BLEND IN WITH THE SURROUNDING AREA
Does the site look natural? Does it attract unwanted attention?

L—LOW-TO-THE-GROUND CONSTRUCTION
Low-to-the-ground construction techniques must be used. Does the site provide protection against small arms and direct weapons fire?

U—UNEXPECTED
Unexpected sites should be used. Will the enemy expect you to look out of the window or small hole in the wall?

E—EVACUATION ROUTES
These must be planned during site selection. Where will you go to link up with your remaining team members if the site is discovered or overrun?

S—SILHOUETTING
Can a sniper see you silhouetted against a skyline, wall, or other object? This problem is avoided if the selected site is on the side rather than the crest of a hill.

26 Urban surveillance

Several key considerations are taken into account when setting up an observation post in an urban area.

COVERT OR DISGUISED?

The most basic consideration is whether this is a completely covert or a disguised mission.

- A unit may be located in an unused building.
- The observation post may be part of a cover or civilian operation in a safe house where people come and go.

▼ LOOKOUT BUDDY

A sniper is often accompanied by a spotter who will look out for possible targets as well as potential threats to the sniper.

HIDDEN POSITION

Brownfield sites can provide a number of possibilities for a covert observation post in a nonpermissive (unfriendly) environment:

- Disused warehouses
- Factory chimneys
- Attics
- Embankments
- Derelict areas covered in undergrowth

Whichever site is eventually chosen, the team must make sure that the area is as safe as possible from attack with options for escape.

27 Safe house

A normal house in an urban area may be used as a safe house for covert surveillance operations.

Special Forces must take care to ensure that:
- There is no unusual activity in and around the house that will attract attention
- There are no unusual deliveries or extra amounts of food
- Windows and doors are not used at strange times of day

The surveillance team also needs to be aware of Electronic Counter Measures that could be used by local or enemy forces.

▼ STAYING SAFE

Special Forces leave a safe house in Kunduz, Afghanistan after an operation.

SPYING ON OSAMA BIN LADEN

Prior to the raid on bin Laden by U.S. Special Forces from SEAL Team 6 in May 2011, the Central Intelligence Agency (CIA) Special Activities Division set up a safe house in Abbotabad to carry out surveillance of the likely lair of Osama bin Laden.

CIA agents moved into the safe house months before the military attack and built up a comprehensive picture of movements to and from bin Laden's house.

VEHICLE SURVEILLANCE

Special Forces surveillance includes using special reconnaissance units to follow targets by road. This type of operation requires several vehicles and a high level of coordination between them.

STAKEOUT

There may be no way of knowing which direction a parked target vehicle will take when a suspect decides to move off. Therefore the stakeout arrangement should provide a number of options in all possible directions so that the target can be followed immediately whatever direction they take.

FOUR OPTIONS

- At a four-way intersection, pursuit vehicles are positioned facing in all four possible directions.
- When the suspect approaches his or her car, one of the stakeout vehicles may pull out in front of the target vehicle to alert the other stakeout vehicles that the target is about to move off.

FLOATING BOX TECHNIQUE

The floating box is a key technique used in vehicle surveillance operations. Once a target car is underway it is impossible to know which way it will turn. There is a danger that:

- A surveillance car may not have time to turn in the same direction
- The movements of surveillance cars following every move of the target car may become too obvious

To operate the floating box technique two or more surveillance cars must work in tandem. The technique often works well in modern urban areas with a good road system.

1 The target vehicle is traveling on road A. Surveillance cars travel on parallel roads B and C to the left and right.

2 If the target turns off road A and moves on to road B or road C, one of these surveillance vehicles can then pick up the pursuit and become the primary tracking vehicle.

The floating box technique requires a high level of communication between the surveillance vehicles, as well as practice.

28 Electronic spying

Special Forces use airborne surveillance via Unmanned Aerial Vehicles (UAVs) and are also linked indirectly into UAV technology, surveillance, and strike assets.

GENERAL ATOMICS MQ-9 REAPER

This UAV was developed to perform high-level surveillance, but also has a hunter-killer role. The aircraft has a powerful onboard camera and is equipped with Hellfire air-to-ground missiles and Sidewinder air-to-air missiles, along with the GBU-12 Paveway II laser-guided bomb.

▼ MO-9 REAPER KEY DATA

Length: 36 ft (11 m)
Wingspan: 65 ft (20 m)
Powerplant: Honeywell TPE331-10 turboprop
Max speed: 555 mph (893 km/h)
Endurance: 14 hours
Armament: AGM-114 Hellfire missiles
    GBU-12 Paveway II laser guided bombs
    GBU-38 Joint Direct Attack Munition (JDAM)
Avionics: AN/DAS-1 MTS-B Multi-Spectral
    Targeting System
    Raytheon SeaVue Marine Search Radar

BOEING SCANEAGLE

The ScanEagle is a portable surveillance UAV that can be operated directly by Special Forces in the field or at sea. The UAV is launched from a catapult and retrieved using a hook and wire system. The ScanEagle carries a high-resolution camera, an infrared camera, a video system, and a micro-synthetic aperture radar.

▼ DOUBLE THREAT

UAVs such as the MQ-9 Reaper not only gather valuable intelligence but can also be used to attack enemy positions.

◀ LIGHT AND PORTABLE

The ScanEagle can provide vital intelligence without compromising the safety of the operator.

29 Surveillance in the field

Special Forces adapt surveillance sites in the field to the particular conditions of different types of landscape—including mountains, forests, deserts, jungles, and swamps.

MOUNTAINS

In mountainous areas, Special Forces will look to take advantage of natural protection. This includes rocks and inlets—as well as tree cover, depending on the position of the hide relative to the tree line.

DESERTS

- In deserts soldiers can conceal themselves and their vehicles behind berms and dunes. Special Forces teams from the United States, U.K., and Australia deployed vehicles in the Iraqi desert during the 2003 war.

- Deserts can sometimes be flat and stony, meaning a team could be in danger of being seen from a great distance.
- Water supply is also a major issue.
- Mirages can affect the ability to identify targets. Observation teams often choose the early morning when the air is clearer to observe their targets.

▼ **LOOK OUT. WATCH OUT.**

Special Forces often carry out surveillance in remote areas but need to be on their guard against being compromised.

SPECIAL RECONNAISSANCE

60

FOREST

- There are many places to conceal a surveillance site in the forest.
- The edge of a tree line is usually an excellent position from which to view the surrounding area.
- When setting up a surveillance site, take care to conceal all signs of approach and to camouflage it effectively after the site has been dug.

JUNGLE AND SWAMP

- Jungles provide many opportunities to conceal a surveillance hide but have limited fields of vision.
- A particular challenge in jungle conditions is that the enemy may also be concealed only feet away—and therefore high levels of vigilance are necessary.

▲ HIDDEN THREAT

Jungle areas provide excellent opportunities for concealment but an enemy may also be concealed nearby.

NIGHT AND DAY

- A hide suitable for nighttime observation is likely to be situated at a good height and have a wide field of vision, but may not be suitable for daytime observation because its position is too exposed.
- In this situation Special Forces will establish two hides. The bottom hide can be occupied during the day and the top hide at night.

6 NAVIGATION

Whether working in small teams or on their own Special Forces troops need high-level navigation skills. Apart from regular map and compass work, soldiers are trained to find their way when normal navigational aids are not available—such as when carrying out escape and evasion. Navigation is also key to providing accurate coordinates for enemy positions.

30 Map and compass

The two main compass types used by Special Forces are the baseplate and the prismatic type. The advice given here is based on a baseplate compass (see over the page).

You should orient the map with the compass as a first step before using them for navigation.

ORIENTING THE COMPASS (BELOW)

1 Rotate the compass housing until the dial reads N (000 degrees).
2 Holding the compass level, wait for the needle to point to magnetic north.
3 Turn the compass so that the needle is in alignment with the orienting arrow. Ensure that the compass needle is not attracted by any nearby metal. The direction of travel for the compass is now magnetic north.

FINDING TRUE NORTH

1 Rotate the compass housing so that the N for north indicated on the dial lies over the index mark for the direction of travel arrow.
2 Adjust the orienting arrow on your compass by either adding west declination or subtracting east declination.
3 Rotate the compass so that the compass needle is aligned with the orienting arrow. The arrow indicating direction of travel will now be pointing toward north.

FINDING GRID NORTH

Follow the same method as for finding true north. The declination correction is the difference between magnetic north and grid north. This figure should be found on your map.

SETTING A MAP

A map that is oriented with the ground will be much easier to use. The map can be set either by using a compass or by using landmarks.

SETTING THE MAP WITH A COMPASS

1 Once you have found either true or grid north with the compass and made the adjustment for declination, place the compass on the map, with the edge of the compass parallel to the grid lines on the map. The direction-of-travel arrow should be pointing toward the north edge of the map.
2 Rotate the map and compass together so that the north end of the compass needle is in alignment with the orienting arrow.

SETTING A MAP BY USING LANDMARKS

1 Look out for a prominent feature.
2 Move the map so that an imaginary line could be drawn from you, through the portrayal of the feature on the map, to the feature itself in front of you.
3 Check other features around you against the map and confirm their relationship to each other. This should give you more confidence that you know where you are.

▲ STEER CLEAR OF METAL

When using a compass, keep clear of metallic objects such as weapons that will have a magnetic effect on the needle.

31 Baseplate compass

The baseplate compass is the most commonly used and is the easiest type of compass to use when orienting with a map.

1 Housing The magnetic needle rotates here and points to figures indicated on a rotary bezel.

2 Baseplate Includes a ruler that can be used for measuring scale.

3 Needle The needle floats in liquid and when the compass is held level, away from any other metal objects, it will always point to magnetic north. In this picture, it is aligned with the **orienting arrow** beneath.

4 Index line Marked on the outer edge of the compass housing and marks the bearings set by rotating the compass housing.

5 Orienting lines These lines rotate when the housing is rotated and can be aligned with the eastings on a map. Eastings are the map gridlines running north/south that measure distance east/west. The orienting lines usually include a red arrow that can be aligned with the eastings or with the compass needle.

6 Direction-of-travel arrow Either shows the direction you want to travel or your bearing.

7 Compass scale Marked on the edge of the base plate and helps you to measure distance on a map.

32 Improvised compass

In an emergency, a Special Forces soldier can improvise a compass.

MAKING AN IMPROVISED COMPASS

1 Magnetize a piece of metal like a sewing needle by stroking it slowly against a magnet. Alternatively, stroke it against a material such as silk.
2 Hang the needle from a thread so that it is evenly balanced. If you have no thread, place the needle on a piece of material or a leaf.
3 In place of a needle you can use a razor blade, which can be stroked in the same way and then suspended from a thread.

The improvised compass may provide a fairly reliable indication of the direction but it is advisable to also use other direction-finding methods—such as checking against the sun—as a backup.

▼ **EMERGENCY NAVIGATOR**
Magnetized pins or needles can be used to make an improvised compass.

▼ **LOCATE POSITION**
A military prismatic compass enables the user to take bearings on geographical landmarks.

USING A WATCH AS A COMPASS

You can use a watch instead of a compass to determine true north and south.

IN THE NORTHERN HEMISPHERE (RIGHT)

1 Point the hour hand toward the sun (shown with a white arrow).
2 Draw an imaginary line between the hour hand and 1200 hours.
3 The north line will be found halfway between hour hand and 1200 hours.

Remember that the sun is in the east before noon and in the west after noon.

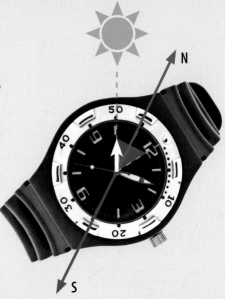

IN THE SOUTHERN HEMISPHERE (LEFT)

1 Point the 1200 dial at the sun.
2 The north line will be found halfway between 1200 hours and the hour hand (shown with a white arrow).

33 GPS

A Global Positioning System (GPS) receiver measures the time it takes radio signals to travel from four or more satellites to its location. It calculates the distance to each satellite and determines the longitude, latitude, and altitude of the person holding the receiver.

CIVILIAN GPS

- GPS was originally developed for military use. Information is displayed in either geographic or military grid coordinates.
- It also has many civilian uses—for example, in your mobile phone or car GPS.

MILITARY USES OF GPS

- Precise direction-finding for military personnel and weapons systems: Navigation and locating position, weapons, targets, and sensors.
- Computing time to the next checkpoint.
- Coordinating firepower, scout, and screening operations.
- Supply operations and identification of obstacles.
- In training programs it provides a central commander with tracking information such as routes taken by soldiers, errors in route finding, and potential for recovery of lost and injured soldiers.

◀ WARNING: LOW BATTERY
A GPS receiver is useful for navigation and pinpointing your position but it depends on batteries so make sure you know how to use a fallback system.

34 Reading the landscape

Intuition and common sense can help you to read the landscape, whether or not you have a map and compass.

JUDGING DIRECTION

- Watch out for snow patches remaining on mountainsides in spring—these are likely to be on the northern side of the slope.
- Look for moss or lichen on trees and boulders—this, too, is normally on the northern side.
- Notice the way trees are bent by the wind— do you know which direction the prevailing wind blows?
- Do you know the countryside you're walking in? If so, you may know—for example—the direction in which mountain ranges and valleys run.

DESERT WINDS

- If you're in the desert, you can get a sense of direction by knowing that the sand dunes are sometimes in alignment with the prevailing winds—if you know the direction of the wind, you can work out the direction of the dunes.
- Other types of dune run at right angles to the direction of the wind. Look out for a shallow upwind slope and steep downwind slope.

READ YOUR SURROUNDINGS
An experienced soldier will interpret natural signs in order to determine direction.

35 Pacing and timing

Pacing is a method of calculating how far you have gone based on the number of steps you have taken. It is an important skill to learn when finding your way around with a map and compass.

KNOW YOUR PACE

- To pace accurately you need to have measured how many paces or double paces you walk in each 100 yards or 100 meters.
- Walk normally when measuring your pacing.
- You'll benefit from learning double pacing. This means you don't have to count so much.

▲ COUNT DOUBLE

Double pacing halves your work. Instead of counting every step, just count steps on one foot.

TYPICAL PACING

- Estimated pacing for an average person is 65 double paces every 100 yards or 100 meters.
- Adjust this if you're walking on slopes or in rough country. Up steep slopes, your pace will shorten dramatically.

HOW LONG WILL IT TAKE?

Estimate how fast you are walking to help work out the length of time it will take to reach your target location.

- If you walk at an average speed of 3 mph (roughly 5 km/h), it should take you around 75 seconds to cover 100 yards (just over a minute for 100 m).
- A distance of about 800 yards should take you about 10 minutes (roughly 9 minutes for 800 m). The time will be affected by slopes, rough ground, and so on.

36 Contouring

Contour lines on a map are drawn between points of the same height. In order to save energy and time, a Special Forces soldier may choose to follow the contours around a landscape feature rather than go up and down—or vice versa.

STRAIGHT OR ROUND?

The direct route may not be the easiest, quickest, or safest. The terrain may be exceptionally rough, and going direct may also expose you to adverse weather conditions.

STUDY THE MAP CAREFULLY

Steep features are marked by contour lines in close proximity. It is usually straightforward to estimate the level of challenge involved by the terrain. When planning your route you will also need to take into account:

- Your level of fitness
- The amount of equipment you are carrying

CONTOURS

Spaced widely—indicate gentle slopes
Spaced close together—indicate steep slopes
No contours—suggests flat ground
Several contours meeting together in a line—signals a vertical cliff.

▼ DON'T CUT CORNERS

Following the contours around a hill can often be easier than taking a straight line over it.

DEAD RECKONING

Dead reckoning—or deduced reckoning—is the calculation of position by estimating distance traveled and direction from a previously determined position or "fix." It provides an accurate method of finding your way over short distances in areas where there are few other clues to work with, such as:

- A desert
- Places with dense foliage—a jungle
- When weather conditions such as fog, mist, or blizzards obscure terrain

▼ **TAKE NOTE: KNOW WHERE YOU ARE**

Dead reckoning is a method of navigation that can be used in areas where visibility is limited.

KEEP NOTES

The process of dead reckoning consists of keeping a note of your movements, including direction and distance. This means regular checks on the compass direction and also an accurate record of pacing.

DEAD RECKONING RECORD

A record of dead reckoning on a journey might look like this:

Time	Course	Distance
0800	090	3 miles (5 km)
0900	035	1 mile (3 km)
11.30	090	2¼ miles (4 km)

37 Taking your bearings

Resection is a method of determining your position by using a compass and a map. It involves taking a bearing on two or more objects or features and then drawing lines to fix your position.

WHERE AM I STANDING?

1 First orient the map using a compass (see page 64).

2 Identify two or more locations visually, and then mark their positions on the map.

3 Use a compass to measure the magnetic azimuth to one of the locations from your own location (see panel opposite).

4 Convert the magnetic azimuth to a grid azimuth, using the conversion figures provided on your map.

5 Create a back azimuth by drawing a line on the map from the location to your own position.

6 Repeat the process for the other location you have identified.

7 Where the lines intersect is your position. Take a note of the grid coordinates.

▼ ESSENTIAL TOOLS
A map and a compass are the basic requirements for successful navigation.

AZIMUTH

- **Magnetic azimuth** is the number of degrees clockwise between magnetic north measured on your compass and a vertical line passing through your target location.
- **Grid azimuth** is the number of degrees clockwise between grid north (on your map) and the vertical line through your target.
- You can convert **magnetic azimuth** to **grid azimuth**, and vice versa, using conversion information provided on your map.

▲ KEEP IN LINE

When taking a bearing with a military prismatic compass look through the sighting slip and line up the hairline in the lid with the object on which the bearing is being taken.

▼ SETTING YOUR MAP

When aligning a compass with a map, the orienting lines in the compass housing are aligned with the grid lines on the map.

38 Navigating by the sun

Special Forces are taught to use the sun in combination with other direction indicators as a means of estimating direction.

In the northern hemisphere, if you can see the sun on a reasonably clear day these tips may help you to get your bearings.

- The sun rises toward the east, reaches its highest point at midday, and sets toward the west.

NORTH VS SOUTH

In the northern hemisphere, the sun will be due south at its highest point in the sky.

In the southern hemisphere, the sun will be due north at its highest point. When you are near the equator, the sun will be almost directly overhead.

- It only rises and sets accurately due east and due west at the equator.

THE SUN VARIES POSITION

The sunrise and sunset positions vary through the year so you can gauge your direction more accurately if you know the following.

- At the spring and autumn equinoxes (March and September) the sun is closest to east and west on the compass.
- At all other times of year there is a variation.
- In mid-summer (the summer solstice) the sun rises in a more north-easterly direction and sets in a north-westerly direction.
- In mid-winter (winter solstice) the sun rises in a more south-easterly direction.

◀ FOLLOW THE SUN
The movement of the sun as it rises in the east and sets in the west is an important navigational aid.

39 Navigating using the moon

When escaping and evading an enemy, Special Forces may choose to travel at night. Apart from the stars, which are a useful navigational tool, a Special Forces soldier may also use the moon.

MOON WALK
As well as the stars, the moon can also be a useful navigational tool at night.

Although the moon is less reliable than the sun as a navigational indicator, due to the angle of its orbit, you can still learn some characteristics of the moon which may be helpful when estimating direction.

FULL MOON

- A full moon rises in the east
- At midnight it is in the south
- A full moon sets in the west

CRESCENT MOON

If there is a crescent moon, imagine a line that runs from the top tip of the crescent to the bottom tip. Where that imaginary line reaches the horizon is roughly due south.

MOON RISE

If the moon rises before the sun has set, the side of the moon reflecting the light of the sun will be facing west. If the moon rises after the sun has set, the side of the moon reflecting the sun will be facing east.

40 Using shadows to tell position and time

You can use the sun to determine direction and tell the time by using a shadow stick.

FINDING DIRECTION WITH A SHADOW STICK

1 Push a stick in the ground so that it casts a shadow.
2 Mark the end of the shadow with a stone or other object. This will mark the west point.
3 Wait for about 15 minutes, until the shadow has moved a few inches.
4 Mark the new position of the shadow with a stone. This identifies the east point.
5 Draw a straight line through the two points in order to create an east-west line
6 Having created this line, you can now work out north and south and directions in between.

TELLING THE TIME WITH A SHADOW STICK

1 Draw a line perpendicular to the east-west line.
2 Place a stick in the ground where the two lines intersect.
3 The shadow cast by the stick can now be used as an hour hand.
4 The east-west line is 0600–1800 hours and the north-south line is the noon line.

▼ WITHOUT A WATCH OR COMPASS?
The shadow-stick method of navigation is a useful and reliable way of estimating direction and time if you do not have a watch or compass.

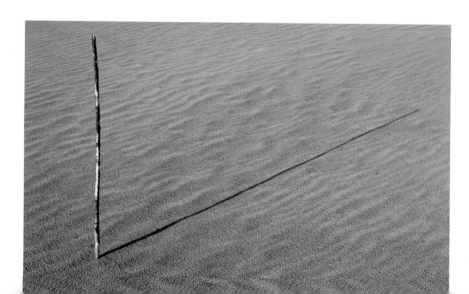

NAVIGATING BY THE STARS

Special Forces soldiers are trained to use the stars for nighttime navigation.

NORTH STAR

The most reliable of all the stars is the North Star, or Polaris, which is almost exactly above true north.

- The position of the North Star relative to the Earth does not change, because the Earth's axis is pointed toward it.
- To locate the North Star, follow a line through the bottom of the pattern of stars known as the Big Dipper (also called the Plough), or from Cassiopeia.

SOUTHERN CROSS

In the southern hemisphere, the arrangement of stars called the Southern Cross is often used to identify south.

- If the Southern Cross is vertical in the sky, south is directly beneath the bottom star.
- If the cross is at an angle, multiply the longest axis of the cross by 4.5, marking an imaginary point above the horizon. South is directly beneath that point.

USING ANY STAR

You can work out direction by checking the movement of any star against a fixed point.

1 You need to stay in one place for 15–20 minutes.

2 Choose a star and identify two fixed points on the ground.

3 Monitor the movement of your chosen star against the fixed points.

4 Work out the direction of the star by one of the following movements:

NORTHERN HEMISPHERE
Rising Star is in the east
Falling Star is in the west
Leftward Star is in the north
Rightward Star is in the south

SOUTHERN HEMISPHERE
Rising Star is in the west
Falling Star is in the east
Leftward Star is in the south
Rightward Star is in the north

◀ FIND THE NORTH STAR
Stars are a useful navigational tool. The most reliable is the North Star, which does not change position.

North Star

Little Dipper

Big Dipper

41 Terrain association

In terrain association you compare what you expect to see from looking at the map to what is actually visible around you.

If necessary you can double check using other methods such as resection (see page 74).

READING THE LANDSCAPE

1 Look for terrain features on the map. There are five major terrain features indicated by contours on a map—hilltop, valley, ridge, depression, and saddle.

2 Look for symbols on the map that show vegetation, such as orchards, coppices, fields, and so on.

3 Check the map for symbols indicating water. They may represent lakes, rivers, or streams.

4 Check the map for man-made features— villages, towns, religious buildings, and so on. You will need to be aware of the age of the map you are using and the possibility that man-made features may have disappeared or that new ones may have appeared that are not recorded on the map.

▼ USE YOUR EYES

Terrain association is a common-sense way of relating features on the ground with those on the map.

AN EYE FOR CHANGE

Terrain features will change through the seasons of the year, depending on which part of the world you are in. Characteristics that may seem clear in one season may not be so clear in another.

- **Snowfall** will make the landscape correspond more closely to the map, despite some features being obscured. Features shown by contour lines on the map may look particularly distinctive.
- **Plant growth** may have the effect of obscuring features and making the terrain less easy to read.
- Once a year, **leaves fall** in abundance.
- If it **rains** a lot, streams and rivers may overflow losing their usual shape.

GEO FEATURES

Special Forces soldiers also take mental note of key terrain features that are either an advantage or disadvantage to themselves or an enemy—including the position of high ground, towns, bridges, and road junctions. They will also look for natural cover and avenues of approach.

▼ AN EVER-CHANGING LANDSCAPE

Terrain may look very different at different times of year and, depending on the age of a map, new features such as a military camp may have appeared.

42 Geographic coordinates

The standard geographic world coordinate system is based on latitudes north or south of the Equator and longitudes east or west of the Prime Reference Meridian of Greenwich.

DEGREES, MINUTES, AND SECONDS

Map and control point references are expressed in degrees (°), minutes ('), and seconds (''); the number of decimal places is a measure of the level of accuracy in pinpointing locations.

COORDINATES

A coordinate system on a map is the grid of intersecting lines that are used to identify a position. Usually these are based on latitude and longitude lines.

▼ CUSTOM MAPS
Military maps may be created at short notice to cover particular areas of operations.

UNIVERSAL TRANSVERSE MERCATOR GRID

The Universal Transverse Mercator (UTM) grid (see below) covers the Earth with lines spaced at a distance of 3,282 feet (1,000 m). There are 60 numbered zones extending north to south.

The UTM grid reference gives the zone number followed by the eastings (distance in meters east of the western edge of the zone) and the northings (distance north of the nearest gridline south of it).

All quadrangle maps made by the U.S. Geological Survey show the UTM grid.

- On 7.5-minute quadrangle maps (a scale of 1:24,000 and 1:25,000) and 15-minute quadrangle maps (scales of 1:50,000, 1:62,500, and 1:63,360), the UTM grid shows intervals of 3,282 feet (1,000 m).
- On maps with a scale of 1:100,000 and 1:250,000, the UTM grid shows intervals of 32,800 feet (10,000 m).
- The intervals are indicated with blue ticks in the map margin or with gridlines.

- You can draw a line through the tick marks to create a latitude line or put on a transparent grid overlay that subdivides the grid for you.
- Using the scale on the map, you can convert into meters the distance between any point on the map and the closet gridline to north/south and east/west.
- Values given at the tick marks allow you to work out the geographical interval. The interval will be 2'30" for 1:25,000 scale maps and 5'00" for 1:50,000 scale maps.
- You can calculate the geographical coordinates of a point on the map by dividing into equal divisions the side of the square in which the point appears.
- With a geographical interval of 5'00," the sides of the geographical square should be divided into 300 equal parts (because 1 minute is 60 seconds, so 5'00"=300") with a value of one second each. This can be measured with a ruler or the edge of a baseplate compass.

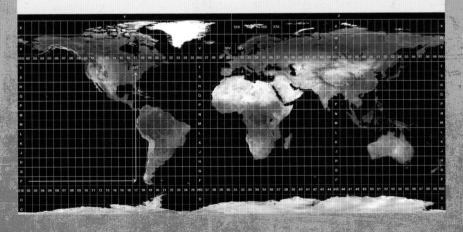

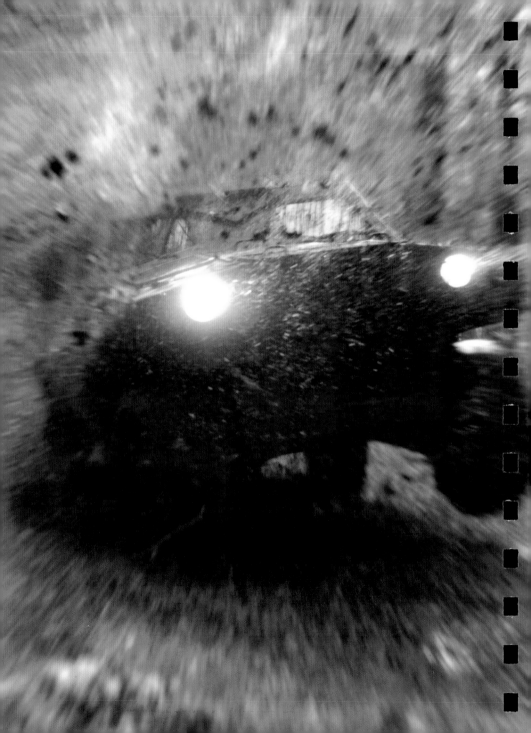

7 DRIVING

Special Forces need to have defensive driving skills to protect themselves and their vehicles, and offensive driving techniques to capture a target or break through a roadblock.

These techniques are illegal and dangerous. You should not attempt these maneuvers yourself.

43 Car handling

Special Forces are taught to drive with maximum awareness. They learn the optimum ways of handling a car on the road and how to achieve the best driving position.

DRIVING POSITION

The driver should be both comfortable and fully in control of the car. The seating position should maximize ability to steer and support the driver during aggressive maneuvers, when the car is likely to roll.

▼ **COVERING ALL THE BASES**
Different types of vehicles have different driving characteristics. Special Forces personnel train in 4x4, front-wheel drive, and rear-wheel drive vehicles.

THE BEST SEAT POSITION

To check the distance between the steering wheel and seat back: Balance your wrists on the top of the steering wheel while keeping your shoulders comfortably in the back of your seat. Then grip the steering wheel with your hands and turn the wheel without taking your shoulders off the back of your seat. At all times, you should have a little bit of flex at the elbows.

44 Driver awareness

Special Forces troops are taught to drive with maximum awareness.

▼ PAY ATTENTION

A "soft-skinned" (unarmored) vehicle on patrol. Maximum awareness is required to keep the driver out of trouble and protect the vehicle.

- Look well ahead in order to gain maximum time to take action in an emergency.
- Use clues in the road to predict how sharp a corner will be or the steepness of a hill.
- Weigh up the least bad option when presented with a hostile roadblock or other obstacle. This may mean making a choice between ramming or attempting to escape over a pavement area.
- When driving at night, take extra care as you will have reduced peripheral vision. Make a conscious effort to scan to the sides of the road to minimize the risk of being taken by surprise.

GETTING OVER AN OBSTACLE

A specialist braking technique helps minimize the impact of obstacles in the road:
- Apply the brakes hard before the obstacle, causing the front of the car to dip downward.
- Release the brakes just before contact with the obstacle. This causes the compressed energy in the suspension system to release, causing the front of the car to lift up again, helping the car over the obstacle.

45 Escaping pursuing vehicles

Special Forces are taught not to get involved in high-speed car chases if they are being followed. They are instructed to attempt an escape in a way that limits their exposure to the pursuit vehicle.

U-TURN

- The Special Forces driver may be able to carry out a U-turn rapidly in front of a pursuing vehicle and then head off at speed in the opposite direction.
- Performing a U-turn may involve going over a curb in the central reservation. Drivers need to practice the art of getting over a curb without damaging the vehicle or getting a flat tire.

SUDDEN STOP

An alternative is high-speed braking.

- The Special Forces driver brings his vehicle to a rapid controlled stop.
- Afterward, the driver may attempt either a Y-turn or a J-turn (see pages 93 and 90).

▼ DOUBLE PROTECTION
A position behind the engine of a car protects a soldier from enemy fire, using the engine as a block as well as the vehicle body.

46 How to identify a potential attack

Taught to be on the lookout for potential attacks, Special Forces watch for unusual behavior and situations. These may involve other vehicles or civilians.

ATTACK ON THE WAY?

Warning signs include:

- Anyone acting nervously
- A person whose behavior seems out of place
- People whose clothing seems unusual for the area
- An unusually empty or quiet area of a town or road
- Vehicles making odd maneuvers
- Any vehicle that may obstruct or hit the driver's vehicle
- A car or motorcycle accident that may have been staged
- Any unexpected detour required from your intended route
- A vehicle following you that has a different style of license plate to local vehicles

▼ ACT FAST

Soldiers dismount quickly to form all-around defense while on vehicle patrol. Quick reactions are required in soft-skinned vehicles.

47 J-turn

The J-turn maneuver involves turning a vehicle that is traveling in reverse so that it travels forward in the same direction.

J-TURN IN A MANUAL CAR

1 Reverse the vehicle at speed.

2 Turn the wheel sharply to start the turn.

3 Press down the clutch and foot brake so that the wheels lock and are no longer engaged with the engine.

4 The momentum of the rear movement and the turn continues to bring the nose of the car round in a 180-degree swing, with the front wheels skidding on the ground.

5 Once the half-turn is complete and the nose is now pointing in the required direction of travel, take one foot off the clutch and the other off the brake, then hit the accelerator to engage the wheels and pull away.

AUTOMATIC J-TURN

To perform this maneuver in an automatic car:

- Halfway through the turn shift into neutral.
- When pointing in the direction of travel shift into Drive.

▼ QUICK GETAWAY

Fast reactions and expert handling of a car in an emergency can mean the difference between life and death for the driver and occupants.

48 Hand-brake turn

The hand-brake turn is similar to the J-turn. The main difference is that the J-turn does not involve the use of the hand brake.

The hand-brake turn is best performed in a saloon or estate car with rear-wheel drive. The maneuver is easier in an automatic vehicle, but it can be effective in a manual car if the driver is well practiced in the technique.

HAND-BRAKE TURN IN AN AUTOMATIC VEHICLE

1 Drive forward at about 35 mph (55 km/h).
2 Take your foot off the accelerator and put the car in neutral.
3 Turn the steering wheel quickly for about one and a half turns. As you begin to turn, engage the hand brake.
4 When the car is sideways on to the original line of travel, release the hand brake.
5 Shift the car from neutral into Drive, hit the accelerator, and turn the steering wheel.
6 Accelerate away.

▼ READY FOR ANYTHING
Special Forces operators undergo training on vehicles with different capabilities, such as this Panther all-terrain vehicle.

HAND-BRAKE TURN IN A MANUAL CAR

1 Drive forward at about 45 mph (70 km/h).
2 Ease off the accelerator and press down on the clutch as you swing the steering wheel around hard, through approximately one and a half turns.
3 As the back of the car slides round, pull up the hand brake.
4 Once the vehicle is facing in the opposite direction to the original line of travel, release the clutch and pull away rapidly, moving quickly through the gears.

J-TURN

91

HAND BRAKE

The hand brake is a hand-operated brake between the driver's seat and the passenger seat, sometimes called a parking brake or e-brake (for "emergency").

49 Braking with the left foot

With this technique the driver performs a maneuver similar to a hand-brake turn, locking the rear wheels with the foot brake.

The driver keeps his right foot on the accelerator while performing the maneuver and places his left foot (normally only used on the clutch pedal in a manual transmission car) on the foot brake.

LEFT-FOOT BRAKING IN A MANUAL CAR

1 Drive forward at about 45 mph (70 km/h).
2 Shift into neutral as you turn the steering wheel rapidly one and a half turns.
3 As the rear of the vehicle begins to slide in response to the sharp turn, jam the foot brake down with your left foot.
4 The effect of applying the brake is that the back of the vehicle should swing around quickly.
5 Shift into first gear and pull away smoothly and rapidly.

SNATCH!

Special Forces use advanced driving techniques in "snatch operations" used to seize a target.

▼ **BEWARE ON SNATCH OPS**
Special Forces operators are trained to remove a target from a vehicle and disarm him. This is a very dangerous operation as the target can easily conceal a weapon inside the car.

50 Y-turn

The Y-turn is one of several rapid reverse and escape turns Special Forces drivers learn to use when faced by a roadblock.

QUICK REVERSE

1 Approach the roadblock in a forward direction.
2 Apply the brakes hard and slow to a stop.
3 Quickly switch to reverse gear.
4 Reverse the car around in a 90-degree turn so that it is sideways to the block.
5 Engage first gear and pull away rapidly, in the opposite direction to the original approach.

STAY CALM

- As with all turns, it is essential to keep as calm as possible and to carry out maneuvers smoothly.
- Be aware of other obstacles.
- Before reversing check that there are no cars behind you.

Y-TURN WITH TWO VEHICLES AND BLOCK BEHIND

When troops in a convoy of two vehicles encounter a roadblock, drivers must coordinate their move to avoid confusion.

- If the road is clear behind the convoy, both cars reverse together, performing a Y-turn in parallel and then pulling away in the opposite direction to their original approach.
- If there is a hostile vehicle behind the two Special Forces cars blocking their reverse, the drivers perform half of the Y-turn, reversing together so that both of the convoy cars are side by side, perpendicular to the original line of approach.
- The drivers leave enough room between their cars to open both sets of doors on the inside. Because the road behind is blocked, there is no option but to escape on foot.
- They get out into the space between the cars, then make their escape if it is safe to move from the cover of the two cars.

▲ DON'T HANG AROUND
To evade and survive a roadblock, a Y-turn is a simple but effective solution, if performed quickly and smoothly.

BOOTLEGGING TURN

This maneuver takes its name from the Prohibition years of the early twentieth century, when bootleggers carrying illegal alcohol had to take evasive action when they encountered a police roadblock.

HOW TO PULL A BOOTLEGGING TURN

1 While the vehicle is traveling forward at speed in a high gear, rapidly engage a low gear (usually second gear) and quickly turn the steering wheel in the direction of the opposite lane.
2 The vehicle skids and the back swings around. Enter the opposite lane.
3 The vehicle should come to a halt facing in the opposite direction from the previous direction of travel, ready to pull away at speed.

▼ A QUICK TURN AROUND

The bootlegging turn is one of the fastest and most effective maneuvers used by Special Forces operators to escape a potentially lethal roadblock. The turn can be performed on an average two-lane road.

51 L-turn

The L-turn is a conventional cornering maneuver when performed at normal speed but you need to be highly skilled to perform it at high speed.

HIGH-SPEED L-TURN

A Special Forces driver who sees an obstacle ahead may choose to quickly turn down a street to the left or right in order to escape. In these circumstances it is very important that the pursuit vehicle is not aware of the driver's intentions.

1 Keep well to the opposite side of the road from the intended direction of turn.

2 Do not give away your intention to turn by applying brakes (and showing brake lights) until the last moment.

3 When the moment comes to make the turn, brake rapidly and turn sharply without causing the vehicle to skid.

4 Make a smooth turn, with the inside edge of the road you are turning into as the apex of the turn and using the far side of that road

to complete the turn (assuming there is no oncoming traffic).

REVERSE 270-DEGREE TURN

This complex turn—performed at speed in reverse—requires a high level of skill. It is used in situations when Special Forces drivers need to get away from an obstacle in front of them, and be ready to escape down a side road.

1 The maneuver starts with the car moving in reverse.

2 Spin the wheel so the car swings around 180 degrees within the same lane. The car is now facing forward.

3 Continue the swing until the car faces at right angles to its original direction of travel. The car is ready to go down a new road.

DON'T TRY THIS AT HOME

HIGHLY TRAINED

Maneuvers described on these pages are only performed by Special Forces personnel who have received advanced driver training and only in circumstances where their lives are in danger. A Special Forces operator would not perform any of these maneuvers in circumstances where they might endanger other drivers or pedestrians.

AUTHORIZED ACCESS ONLY

Apart from highly-trained military or intelligence personnel, the only other organization authorized to carry out selected maneuvers of this kind are the police.

52 Driving through corners

Special Forces drivers are taught the most efficient cornering techniques. These are taken from methods used by racing drivers.

CORNERING: KEY ADVANTAGES

If you can corner more effectively than a driver in a pursuing vehicle you have a substantial advantage.

- Taking the correct line through a corner means you can maintain maximum speed and forward momentum with the least amount of roll.
- Your car will be able to pull out of the corner and pick up speed more efficiently.

WATCH OUT FOR OTHER DRIVERS

When taking a racing line through a corner, drivers need to be aware of other road users, especially those coming the other way.

HOW TO TAKE A CORNER

1 Brake and change down a gear or more before the corner and while the vehicle is still traveling in a straight line.
2 Identify the apex of the bend and steer toward it, while accelerating gently to keep the car stable.
3 On reaching the apex of the bend, identify the exit point of the corner and head toward that, maintaining steady acceleration.
4 On reaching the exit point of the corner, accelerate harder to pull the car away at speed.

▼ DRIVE FAST. DRIVE WELL.
Military scout vehicles are often either open vehicles or driven with the windows open for maximum visibility.

53 Opposite lock

The opposite lock is a spectacular way of engaging corners, often seen in action films or rally driving. With this technique you can maintain momentum while taking a vehicle fast around a bend.

The opposite lock technique is only used in rear-wheel drive vehicles, and where the surface of the road is relatively loose or dry.

COUNTERSTEERING

Opposite lock is also called countersteering because you have to steer as far as you can in the opposite direction—steer left when you are taking a right bend and right on a left bend.

BEAT THE BEND

1 When approaching the bend, turn the wheel quickly into the bend in order to create a lateral movement at the rear of the vehicle.
2 Keep accelerating. This increases the lateral movement at the rear.
3 Apply opposite lock with the steering wheel in order to stabilize the skid.
4 On reaching the bend, accelerate further. This will control the vehicle through the bend.

▼ ONE FOR THE PROFESSIONALS

Opposite lock is a highly skilled method of engaging a bend, often employed by rally drivers and by trained Special Forces operators.

54 Precision Immobilization Technique (PIT)

This maneuver is used by law enforcement vehicles when pursuing another vehicle to force the vehicle in front to stop.

PIT DRIVING

Car A is pursuing car B.

1 Car A partially overtakes car B to the point at which car A's nose (forward of its front wheels) is aligned with car B's rear (behind its back wheels).

2 Car A's driver gradually moves car A closer to car B. When the two cars are touching, car A's driver makes a sharp turn in the direction of car B.

3 As car B begins to lose control and to skid, car A continues the turn so that it moves past car B on the opposite side to the first contact.

HIGHLY DANGEROUS

At speed, the PIT maneuver can be highly dangerous and lead to a fatal accident. A police officer in a pursuing vehicle will only attempt the maneuver in circumstances where other road users will not be endangered and where there is reasonable space for the other vehicle to lose control and come to a halt.

TAKING CONTROL OF A VEHICLE IF THE DRIVER IS INJURED

When two Special Forces operators are traveling together, there may be an emergency—for example, the driver may be injured by gunfire while the car is still moving. The passenger must act quickly to take control of the vehicle to avoid a crash.

- The first thing to do is take control of the steering wheel. If the passenger is wearing a seat belt, he will hold the steering wheel steady with one hand until he has released the belt. Then he will lean across the immobilized driver to grab the wheel with both hands.

- If the vehicle is speeding because the immobilized driver still has his foot on the accelerator, the passenger may either pull the gear lever into neutral, or pull the driver's leg away from the accelerator pedal.

- If the vehicle is in neutral it will naturally slow to a stop.

- It may be possible for the passenger to get his foot across to the brake pedal to slow the car. This will depend on the design of the car and whether it has a major division between the passenger and driver foot wells.

- The alternative is just to pull the gear lever into neutral and pull on the handbrake.

This technique is used when a Special Forces operations vehicle needs to force its way through a roadblock formed by other vehicles.

WHEN TACTICAL RAMMING WORKS

- Tactical ramming is only likely to be successful where the opposing vehicle is to some degree side-on to the ramming vehicle.
- The blocking vehicle may be moving while it attempts to block your path. It is important to ram the opposing vehicle at the rear of its direction of travel—the rear side of the vehicle if it is moving forward and the front side if it is moving backward.
- Hit the opposing vehicle with only the left or right side of the front of your vehicle. This reduces the chances of an impact that might bring your vehicle to a halt.

▼ PREPARE FOR IMPACT

Tactical ramming techniques are practiced by Special Forces operators so that they have a chance of surviving the impact.

NOT TOO FAST!

If you attempt ramming at too high a speed, you may end up in a crash that puts your vehicle out of action.

HOW TO PERFORM TACTICAL RAMMING

- Approach the target vehicle at slow speed. This may confuse your opponent—they may think you are about to stop.
- Align your vehicle at the correct angle for a glancing blow. Aim at the rear side of a forward-moving vehicle, the front side of a reversing vehicle.
- When about the length of your vehicle away from the target, accelerate hard toward the intended point of impact.

BREACHING A BARRICADE

Special Forces are taught this method for breaching a barricade. The technique is similar to that for tactical ramming.

ONE-CAR BARRICADE

1 Slow the car as you approach the roadblock.
2 Change into a lower gear.
3 Wait until your car is about two car lengths from the block, then apply the brakes hard. This makes the front of the car dip downward.
4 Aim for the right rear wheel arch of one of the blocking cars.
5 Wait for the front of your car to lift upward due to the release of energy from the suspension, then accelerate toward the desired point of impact.
6 While accelerating, keep a hand on the gear lever to stop the car slipping out of gear.

TWO-CAR BARRICADE

A barricade of two vehicles is more complex. As the driver you need to make a quick decision on which vehicle to lift and think of any potential knock-on effects of the impact.

- **Aim for the rear** Faced with two vehicles sideways on, you may decide to hit one vehicle in the rear wheel arch, as with the single-car barricade, and move on. This will shunt one blocking vehicle into the other. But this maneuver is difficult to perform if the blocking vehicle is jammed against the pavement and it may also cause the two blocking cars to lock together.
- **Go for the middle** An alternative approach is to aim for the middle of the car barricade, which should have the effect of pushing both cars aside simultaneously.

◀ BE AGGRESSIVE

Military vehicles at a check point in Iraq. Special Forces are trained to engage aggressively with a road block rather than attempting to drive around it, as this is likely to expose them to gunfire from the enemy manning the roadblock.

8 VEHICLES, AIRCRAFT, AND MARITIME CRAFT

Special Forces vehicles range from specialized all-terrain vehicles to specially adapted helicopters and unique watercraft. In some cases vehicles are specifically designed for the unique demands of Special Forces missions.

56 Ambush protection

Mine-resistant vehicles can help avoid fatalities in theaters of war where soft-skinned vehicles are attacked with Improvised Explosive Devices (IEDs).

ON THE MOVE

Mine-Resistant Ambush Protected Vehicles (MRAP) are used for transporting troops and mission support with onboard communications and computer systems. Special Operations Command (SOCOM) variants are fitted with a remote weapons system. As an operative, you can fire without having to show yourself in the open.

THICK SKIN

As well as being mine-resistant, MRAP vehicles are protected against attack from medium-range and small-arms fire.

▼ RG 333 KEY DATA

Manufacturer: BAE Systems Land Systems South Africa
Length: 22.1 ft (6.5 m)
Width: 8 ft (2.4 m)
Height: 9.5 ft (2.9 m)
Engine: Cumming 400 16 Diesel HP
Speed: 68 mph (109 km/h)
Armament: Remote weapon station

▼ TOUGH ENOUGH
MRAP vehicle on a scouting mission in Afghanistan.

57 All-terrain transport—M-ATV

The MRAP all-terrain vehicle (M-ATV) is a replacement for the standard soft-skinned military transport, the M1114 HMMWV or Humvee.

▲ DESIGNED TO LAST

A Special Forces Ground Mobility Vehicle on patrol. These are beefed-up versions of the standard M114 HMMWV.

TOUGH AND POWERFUL

The MRAP-ATV Special Forces variant is a compact, highly mobile, and adaptable transport system. It provides protection from mines and IEDs. The TAK-4 independent suspension system provides maximum mobility over rough terrain. It has a 7.62 mm M240 machine gun with optional remote control, grenade launcher, or M2 Browning heavy machine gun.

GROUND MOBILITY VEHICLE

The GMV is another development of the Humvee, specially adapted for use by Special Forces and elite regiments.

GMV: KEY IMPROVEMENTS AND ADAPTATIONS

- Improvements over the standard version of the Humvee include better ground clearance, more rugged suspension and tires, and a more powerful engine.
- The GMV can be adapted to take a range of armaments such as the Browning M2 .50 mm heavy machine gun, M240 7.62 mm machine gun, M249 SAW 5.56 mm machine gun, and MK19 or MK47 40 mm grenade launcher.
- It also carries smoke-grenade launchers designed to provide concealment when breaking contact with the enemy.

58 Compact all-terrain transport

All-terrain vehicles (ATVs) such as the Polaris MV700 and MV800 are the most compact means of off-road transport—other than a motorbike. They are rugged all-wheel-drive vehicles with run-flat tires that still function after being punctured.

HIGH PERFORMERS

These vehicles can carry up to two people and equipment on a flatbed rack at the rear with fold-down sides, D-rings, and tie-downs. They come in four- or six-wheel variants and have motorbike-style handlebars. To increase adaptability in areas where fuel type cannot be predicted, the ATV can run on either diesel, gasoline, or JP8 (military diesel). The vehicle's headlight can be switched to infrared when necessary.

MISSION TASKS

The ATV can be used to pull trailers with extra equipment. They are fitted with winches on the front that can be used to help the vehicle out of difficult driving areas and to winch in other objects.

▼ A QUICK LIFT

Small all-terrain vehicles (ATVs) have proved popular and useful for moving Special Forces operators, such as this sniper on the back, quickly across rugged terrain.

59 Rapid response vehicles

The Cougar 6x6 is a multi-purpose armored patrol vehicle that can carry ten passengers in a highly secure environment with armor protection from mines, IEDs, and small-arms fire.

The Cougar and related vehicles are used extensively by ordnance bomb disposal teams and are employed by Special Forces in reconnaissance and urban response. The vehicles have been proven to save lives in battle.

▲ SPECIALLY ADAPTED
A camouflaged Land Rover on patrol. Its formidable armament includes a 7.62 mm general-purpose machine gun on the bonnet and an anti-armor weapon on the side.

MASTIFF
The British version of the Cougar 6x6 is the Mastiff. This vehicle is fitted with the British BOWMAN communications system as well as electronic countermeasures equipment.

The Mastiff can be fitted with a 7.62 mm general-purpose machine gun (GPMG), a 12.7 mm heavy machine gun, and a 40 mm grenade machine gun.

RIDGEBACK
The Ridgeback Protected Patrol Vehicle (PPV) is the British equivalent of the Cougar 4x4. This is a highly mobile protected vehicle that can be fitted with Enforcer remote-weapons stations.

60 Patrol vehicles

DESERT PATROLLER

An adapted version of the standard Land Rover 110, the Land Rover 110 Desert Patrol Vehicle features coil springs, four-wheel drive based on that used in the Range Rover, with a two-speed transfer gear box and lockable central differential. The 110 refers to the 110 inch (280 cm) length of the wheel base.

The Desert Patroller was used by British Special Forces, including the Special Air Service, in the wars in the Gulf. In such operations, it can be adapted to carry the large array of specialist communications equipment and armament required for a Special Forces mission.

▼ DAY OF THE JACKAL

A Jackal armored vehicle is mine-resistant but otherwise depends on speed, mobility, and fire power for protection.

OPEN POSITION

The Jackal has a relatively open driving and gun position. The idea is that good all-around visibility and wide arcs of fire, as well as mobility and agility, are the best forms of protection on this kind of vehicle.

JACKAL

The Supacat HMT 400 "Jackal" is fitted with both mine and ballistic armor. The air-suspension system allows for stable ride and is adjustable for height, allowing the vehicle to be loaded into a CH-47 Chinook helicopter. It can be fitted with mission-specific communications equipment and weapons.

PINKIES

BUSHMASTER

The Bushmaster Infantry Mobility Vehicle (IMV) is built in Australia and is in service with the Australian and British armies. It is used by the British Special Air Service (SAS).

It can carry nine soldiers and their equipment, as well as fuel and supplies for three days. It is fitted with armor to deflect mine and ballistic attacks and is based on a V-hull monocoque. The vehicle has one front and two rear hatches where medium and light machine guns can be mounted.

British versions of the Bushmaster have a remote firing system that enables the heavy machine gun to be controlled from inside the vehicle. It can also carry 40 mm Heckler & Koch grenade launchers.

PANHARD VPS

This is a light patrol vehicle used by French Special Forces. It is fitted with a mine-resistant floor and is capable of operating in extreme temperatures. The vehicle is based on the Mercedes-Benz 270 CDI G-Class. The VPS can carry four personnel, including the driver, and can take a 12.7 mm heavy machine gun at the rear and a 7.62 mm light machine gun at the front.

LAND ROVER PERENTIE 6X6 LONG RANGE PATROL VEHICLE (LRPV)

This vehicle is a development of the Land Rover 110 adapted specially for the Australian Special Air Service Regiment (SASR). It is fitted with a front live axle with coil springs, while the rear suspension consists of leaf springs.

The Perentie LRPV carries two spare wheels on either side of the body. It is powered by a 4-cylinder Isuzu diesel engine. Armament includes machine gun mounts at the back and front of the vehicle. It can also be fitted with the Javelin missile system. Special Forces soldiers can hang their personal equipment such as rucksacks over the front and rear of the vehicle and on the sides.

PERENTIES ON MISSION

61 Specialist motorcycles

Special Forces operatives often use specially adapted military models of commercial motorcycles for long-range reconnaissance.

HARLEY-DAVIDSON MT

The Harley-Davidson MT350E motorcycle is a development of the Armstrong MT500. In service, you would use this for reconnaissance and support for Special Forces missions. It is fitted with a carrier for a weapon as well as a document carrier. It has a Rotax 348 cc air-cooled single-cylinder four-stroke engine with a single overhead cam.

KAWASAKI M1030

The M1030 is a military version of the commercial Kawasaki KLR 650 motorcycle. The U.S. Marine Corps and other services use it. A NATO-adapted version, known as the M1030M1E, is used by the United Kingdom and other countries.

LIGHT AND MOBILE

Why pick a motorcycle for reconnaissance?
- You can take the motorcycle offroad, where you are less likely to encounter explosives.
- It is less easy to spot than a large military vehicle, making it less likely that you'll be seen by the enemy.
- Motorcycles allow you to ride into areas otherwise only accessible by foot.
- Bikes are fast and maneuverable so you can get out of trouble quickly.

◀ AGILE AND QUICK
Motorcycles are sometimes employed by Special Forces for reconnaissance and as back-up for heavier vehicles.

COVERT VEHICLES

Operating on a covert mission in a non-conflict environment you often need to maintain a low-key presence.

LOOKING NORMAL

Special Forces often choose vehicles that will merge with their environment and be outwardly typical of the type seen in a particular area. For example in central Asia, these include the Mitsubishi Pajero, Toyota Hilux, Land Rover Defender, and Toyota Prado in both sport and pickup versions.

HIDDEN MIGHT

The casual observer will not be able to distinguish these special operations vehicles from their civilian counterparts, but beneath their benign exterior is heavy armor plating, strengthened suspension, enhanced brake systems to handle the extra weight, advanced communications equipment, and powerful weapons.

QUIET APPROACH

Members of the British Special Boat Service made an appearance at Qala-i-Jhangi fortress, northern Afghanistan, in 2001 to help quell an uprising among Taliban prisoners. They drove white Land Rover Defenders in order to be as inconspicuous as possible.

▼ BLEND IN

At first glance a standard SUV, this vehicle includes armor plating and bullet-proof glass, strengthened suspension and brakes, and advanced communications equipment.

62 Air reconnaissance

The All Environment Capable Variant (AECV) Puma is a mini reconnaissance aircraft designed to land near vertically on either land or water.

STEADY CAMERA

The Puma delivers high image quality. It has image tracking and image stabilization. Its image stabilization technology means that it can maintain a regular image of a particular area, despite fluctuations in its flight pattern.

EASY LAUNCH

The Puma is highly portable. Even as an operator working solo, you can launch it from land or from a boat.

REMOTE CONTROL

You can control the Puma from a Ground Control Station. It carries an onboard GPS system for accurate navigation and positioning.

MAXIMUM RESULT. MINIMUM RISK.

A portable reconnaissance aircraft such as the Puma can provide valuable information about enemy movements with minimal risk.

63 Direct action helicopters

The UH-60 Black Hawk helicopter is the standard U.S. military tactical transport helicopter. MH-60 variants were developed specifically for special operations, to be flown by the U.S. Army's 160th Special Operations Aviation Regiment.

MH-60: KEY FEATURES

- In-flight refueling probe
- AN/APQ-174B terrain-following radar
- Better weapons capability
- Defensive array

PENETRATOR

The MH-60L Direct Action Penetrator (DAP) is equipped with stub wings that can carry M230 Chain Gun 30 mm automatic cannon and rocket pods. M134D Miniguns are placed in the door areas.

▲ COLLECTION POINT

A UH-60 Black Hawk helicopter lands in a field to extract soldiers. The open landscape makes this a relatively safe rendezvous, reducing the risk of an ambush.

64 Heavy-lift helicopters

The MH-47 Chinook is the standard heavy-lift dual-rotor helicopter for U.S., U.K., and other armed forces. Some Chinooks have been adapted for special operations to improve their capabilities.

MH-47E: KEY FEATURES

- Integrated adverse-weather digital cockpits
- Forward-looking infrared terrain-following/avoidance radar
- Long-range fuel tanks and air-refueling probe
- Low-level high-speed flight for carrying troops in or out of a mission area at night or in adverse weather

MH-47G: ADAPTATIONS

The MH-47G has all the capabilities of the MH-47E, plus:

- Improved avionics (electronic systems for communication, navigation, and so on) with integrated digital mission management
- Aircraft survivability equipment (high-tech machinery and design features to reduce an aircraft's vulnerability to attack) and dual embedded global positioning system

- Redundant navigator for improved accuracy and reliability
- Ability to receive and display Near Real Time Intelligence Data (NRTID)
- More efficient T55-GA-714A turboshaft engine
- Improved airframe structure
- M-134 Gatling Miniguns and M-240D machine guns

▼ UPGRADE

The MH-47G Chinook is a specially adapted variant designed to cope with the severe demands of Special Forces missions.

65 Light helicopters

The AH-6M and MH-6M Mission Enhanced "Little Bird" is a light, highly compact helicopter, based on the design for a reconnaissance helicopter.

▲ DESIGNED FOR SMALL SPACES
An unmanned version of the AH-6 Little Bird helicopter. The manned versions are used regularly by U.S. Special Forces.

U.S. Army special operations strategists recognized the potential for Little Bird in infiltration and extraction operations (dropping and airlifting troops) in restricted spaces.

MH-6M "SIDE SADDLE"

There is only room inside the helicopter for three—including pilot and navigator. External benches were added, one on each side capable of carrying up to three Special Forces troops. Other MH-6M enhancements included external personnel pods (EPS), fast-rope insertion/extraction (FRES) equipment,

motorcycle racks, and a winch system.

AH-6M "SHARPSHOOTER"

Special features include:
- M134 Miniguns
- M260 FFAR rocket pods
- AGM-114 laser-guided anti-tank missiles
- GAU-19 .50 caliber 3-barrel Gatling guns

AH-6M AND MH-6M

Additional features include:
- Six-bladed rotors
- Advanced avionics

66 Specialist aircraft

These aircraft are deployed for close air support to back up ground troops and for urban operations. The tilt-rotor CV-22B Osprey combines the benefits of a helicopter and a conventional aircraft.

AC-130U SPECTRE

Weaponry is on the left or port side of the aircraft. As the pilot you fly the Spectre in a circle around the target area, allowing fire to be maintained by your fellow crew members without interruption. Guns include 25 mm Gatling gun, 40 mm Bofors cannon, and 105 mm cannon.

CV-22B OSPREY

Special Forces adaptations include terrain-following radar, forward-looking infrared sensor, and advanced avionics for low-altitude operations in adverse weather conditions.

▼ CV-22 OSPREY

U.S. Army soldiers with Alpha Company, 4th Battalion, 10th Special Forces Group fast-rope from a CV-22 Osprey tilt-rotor aircraft during an exercise.

67 Medium support and attack helicopters

These multirole battlefield helicopters are used for attack roles as well as infiltration and extraction of Special Forces.

PUMA—SPECIALIST ADAPTATIONS

The helicopter can be fitted with specialist equipment for desert and arctic warfare. It can carry 12 fully equipped soldiers. Equipment includes satellite-based GPS, instrument-landing system for adverse weather, two general-purpose machine guns (GPMGs), and a defensive-aids suite—this system provides protection for airborne platforms with missile-approach warning system and infrared jammer.

LYNX—ADAPTABLE OPERATOR

The Lynx AH.9 can carry up to nine soldiers with all their personal equipment. Armament includes a general-purpose machine gun, miniguns, gun pods, rocket pods, eight HOT Hellfire or TOW missiles. The aircraft has an automatic flight control system (AFCS).

Other features include night-vision-compatible cockpit lighting for covert operations, defensive-aids suite, direct infrared countermeasures, and four fast-rope stations.

▶ **SUPER CHARGED**
Special Forces operators fast-rope on to the deck of a cargo ship from a Eurocopter AS332 Super Puma on a training exercise.

68 Marine vehicles

Special Forces use underwater and surface craft for reconnaissance missions, infiltrating, and extracting operatives.

MARK V SPECIAL OPERATIONS CRAFT

The Mark V compact patrol boat is used for high-speed infiltration and extraction of combat swimmers (see page 126). It can carry up to 16 fully equipped combat swimmers, plus four Combat Rubber Raiding Craft (CRRC), with a mission range 500 miles (800 km).

It has twin MTU 12-cylinder TE94 diesel engines and weapon mounts capable of carrying both small-caliber weapons and M2 .50 caliber heavy machine guns, M240 or M60 7.62 mm machine guns, and MK19 40 mm grenade launchers. It is fitted with a Stinger Air Defense System.

SPECIAL OPERATIONS CRAFT—RIVERINE

This craft is designed for short-range infiltration and extraction of Special Forces on inland-water missions. It is also used for reconnaissance, fire-support, or search and rescue. The craft has two forward and three aft mounts for M60 7.62 mm, MK-19, and M2HB .50 caliber weapons.

RIGID HULL INFLATABLE BOAT

The boat is designed for short-range infiltration and extraction, reconnaissance missions, and direct action. It can carry up to eight Special Forces soldiers and equipment plus a crew of three.

▼ READY TO BOARD
A fast-attack boat of the Norwegian Forsvarets Spesialkommando (Special Forces) deploys a telescopic ladder while practicing ship-boarding techniques.

SWIMMER DELIVERY VEHICLE (SDV)

The SDV is a submersible designed for covert infiltration and extraction in hostile territory (see page 126).

WET TRANSPORT

The SDV is a "wet" transport system. You have to breathe from scuba gear or from the onboard oxygen supply.

119

9 AMPHIBIOUS SKILLS AND GEAR

Amphibious operations are key to many Special Forces missions and can involve attaching limpet mines to enemy vessels or providing advance intelligence for the suitability of main force landings in coastal areas. Special Forces may be dropped by submarine, inflatable or rigid craft, or via swimmer-delivery vehicles.

69 Diver training

U.S. Navy SEALs attend and graduate from Basic Underwater Demolition/SEAL school. The highly demanding course focuses on physical training, water training, mental endurance, and teamwork.

PROVE YOUR FITNESS

Before starting your training you have to pass the Diver / SEAL Physical Screening Test. Minimum requirements include:

- 500 yard (460 m) swim (breast stroke or combat sidestroke) in under 12 minutes 30 seconds
- 42 push-ups in 2 minutes
- 50 sit-ups in 2 minutes
- At least six chin-ups

VISIT TO HELL

The first part of the course is seven weeks' physical conditioning. You are in a boat crew of six to eight men. Each week the training

ADVANCE FITNESS

To pass the diver training course, you have to make sure you are in top physical condition even before you start.

load is increased. You have to perform a 4 mile (6.5 km) timed run, a timed obstacle course, and 2 mile (3.2 km) timed swim.

The fourth week is known as "Hell Week." You face five-and-a-half days of continuous physical activity, including 20 hours physical training per day. You will have no more than four hours of sleep throughout the entire period. You will do 200 miles (320 km) of running in total.

LIVING IN WATER

After Hell Week, you move on to the main specialism for the U.S. Navy SEAL unit, combat diving. You learn how to become a basic combat swimmer along with open- and closed-circuit diving.

BACK ON LAND

The next phase of training is land warfare skills. You learn patrolling, rappelling, and navigation.

▶ GO TO HELL!
U.S. Navy SEAL recruits lie in the surf as part of their basic training during Hell Week.

COULD YOU MASTER THIS?

The final phase of training is SEAL Qualification Training (SQT)—Mastery of SEAL skills. You will be trained in:
- Weapons handling
- Demolitions
- Cold-weather operations
- Maritime operations
- Static-line and free-fall parachute operations
- High Altitude-Low Opening (HALO) and High Altitude High Opening (HAHO) operations
- Survival, evasion, resistance, and escape

123

70 Underwater tests

An important part of diver training are tests in a recompression chamber with scuba rigs and underwater fitness challenges.

RECOMPRESSION

In a recompression chamber you breathe pure oxygen under pressure to test your adaptability.

SCUBA TESTS

You have to perform tasks with scuba rigs in a swimming pool. The challenges are designed to test whether you panic under pressure. They include:

- Tying knots
- Taking off your equipment and swapping it with a partner while underwater

CONFIDENT AND CALM

You need to be confident in your equipment and your own strength to cope with the underwater tests.

▼ UNDERWATER PRESSURE

If you find it difficult to remember how to tie knots, try doing it underwater, with an instructor ready to poke you in the ribs just when you get to that really tricky bit!

▼ OCEAN EPIC

To test your fitness and endurance as a U.S. Navy SEAL you have to swim
5.5 miles (9 km) in the cold ocean, buffeted by waves.

UNDERWATER TESTS

125

FRIEND OR FOE?

As part of these tests, your instructor will
deliberately interfere with your equipment
while you are going through your routines.
This includes pulling out vital oxygen hoses
and removing other pieces of equipment in an
attempt to confuse you.

UNDERWATER ENDURANCE

Another key aspect of scuba training is physical
endurance. You may be called on to swim
great distances underwater, perform a mission
(which may involve fighting), and then swim
back again to base or a submarine vehicle
rendezvous.

71 Sea missions—delivery vehicles

Amphibious Special Forces are infiltrated into and extracted from a conflict zone—or an area where covert operations are required—in several ways.

SWIMMER DELIVERY

A Swimmer Delivery Vehicle (SDV) can be launched from a ship or a submarine fitted with a suitable chamber. It can carry four combat divers into the area of operations. The vehicle has its own air supply so that divers can save their personal air supplies for the active part of the operation. Combat divers carry their own personal weapons.

The SDV is parked near the operational area. Divers swim off to carry out the mission, then swim back to the SDV to carry them back to the base sub or ship.

TAKE FIVE

On some missions divers are delivered to a combat area in the Mark V special operations craft. This has a range of 500 miles (800 km) and can carry 16 combat swimmers and 4 combat rubber raiding craft.

The Mark V is used to carry a Special Forces team into a medium-threat area. Combat swimmers would use a combat rubber raiding craft to enter the area of operations with stealth—usually at night. On board the raiding craft, they stow their weapons under the deck and straddle the sides with their legs.

▼ **HIDDEN APPROACH**

A SDV is designed to carry combat or reconnaissance divers toward their mission area from a warship or submarine.

RIVER MISSIONS

In rivers and other inland waterways, purpose-designed craft may be used such as the Special Operations Craft Riverine (SOC-R).

RIVERINE CRAFT

Capable of high-speed movement in relatively shallow waters, it can carry up to eight operators along with all their personal equipment.

The boat is heavily armed, with a combination of 7.62 mm or .50 caliber machine guns, 40 mm grenade launchers, and 7.62 mm miniguns. It can be beached in mud riverbanks to drop off or pick up Special Forces when necessary.

▲ HIT HARD. HIT FAST.
Speed and hitting power are the main defensive and offensive assets of these craft.

RIVER AMBUSH

It is easy for an enemy to conceal themselves and create an ambush in inland waterways. The Riverine relies on speed and devastating firepower to defend itself.

72 Shallow diving

For close-to-shore shallow-diving infiltration, Special Forces use specialist equipment that eliminates the danger of being identified through the bubbles expelled by standard scuba gear.

REBREATHER

As a combat diver you might use the LAR-V Draeger Rebreather. This is a closed-circuit underwater breathing system that recycles the air you expel from your lungs. When you expel air, the system filters out the carbon dioxide.

You can use it to a depth of 70 feet (20 m), making it ideal for shallow-diving operations. It is compact and worn on your chest. This reduces the likelihood of your being spotted.

SCUBA: PROS AND CONS

- Scuba diving apparatuses can be used on missions that require work at greater depth or for longer periods.
- Its disadvantage is that it leaves a trail of bubbles that can be identified from the surface, either by the naked eye or by infra-red equipment.
- Scuba equipment is also bulky and cannot be worn by a combat diver on land.

DON'T BLOW BUBBLES
Rebreather systems are designed to filter air breathed out of the lungs rather than expelling it into the water, which would create give-away bubbles.

▲ **THE DROP SPOT**
Combat swimmers are often delivered to their mission area in small rubber craft.
After completing the mission, they return to the craft.

AN EXPLOSIVE MISSION

In 1989, U.S. Navy SEAL units destroyed two enemy attack boats in Panama harbor.

IDENTIFY THE TARGET
Wearing LAR-V closed-circuit rebreathers, the SEAL team swam into the harbor undetected, carrying limpet mines and plastic explosives. They identified the two boats and placed the mines on the hull of one boat and plastic explosives around the propeller shaft of the other.

GET CLEAR
They set the explosive timers for about 20 minutes, giving themselves just enough time to swim out of the harbor and locate SEAL members operating a combat rubber raiding craft (CRRC) nearby. As they powered away, both of the enemy boats blew up as planned.

73 Underwater navigation

To get to their location in a shallow-dive operation, combat swimmers need to navigate as accurately as if they were on land.

KICK-COUNT

In these operations you use navigation tools such as compass and GPS. You also learn how to work out your kick-count, just as you count paces when walking (see page 71), so you can determine how far you have swum.

SWIMBOARD

As a combat diver swimming toward your location, you might use a swimboard. These handheld units contain an illuminated compass, a depth gauge, a timer, and watches.

IT TAKES TWO

In a combat-swimmer pair, you might carry the swimboard and focus on navigation while your partner swims above you and to the side, looking out for any potential obstacles and alert for any signs of enemy movement.

▼ KEEP ON COURSE
A combat diver team will take one swimboard holding essential equipment such as a compass and depth gauge.

74 Underwater mining

As a combat swimmer on an explosives mission you carry with you limpet mines to place on the hull of a vessel.

GET YOUR ID RIGHT

On an explosives mission you must make sure you have identified the right vessel. This is difficult in the dark when all you can see is the large hull.

GETTING BACK

To get back on course for the return journey, you have to swim some distance from the vessel so that the magnetic effect of the steel hull no longer affects your navigation equipment.

▲ CHECK YOUR TARGET

A diver maneuvers beneath the hull of a boat, ready to place a training explosive. Often such operations are carried out in the dark and it is vital to identify the correct hull.

INVISIBLE SEALS

In training, U.S. Navy SEALs must successfully perform an underwater mining task without being detected from the surface.

75 Airdrop and beach approach

The key skills for amphibious Special Forces teams are to handle airdropping of troops and equipment and cope with the transition from water to land during missions.

AIR DELIVERY

Operations may involve dropping a raiding craft from an aircraft. Special Forces troops jump and fit engines to the craft. Aboard the craft, they travel toward the target area.

FROM SEA TO LAND

On approaching the beach, the boat's coxswain must take care to keep the engines at idle speed so as not to alert the enemy with the noise. As you approach land, combat divers move into the water.

You might wear a rubber wetsuit with camouflage uniform over the top. Alternatively, you might carry dry camouflage clothing in a sealed bag and, once on the beach, change into dry clothes for the land operation.

FIN FALL

Some Special Forces are trained to free-fall parachute into the sea wearing swim fins.

CLIMBING

You may not have the luxury of landing on a sandy beach. If your mission involves scaling a cliff, you'll have to quickly transition to advanced climbing skills. Climbing a cliff is difficult enough when you have dry equipment and clothing; it is even more difficult if your equipment and clothing is cold and wet.

ON THE LOOKOUT

While some operators change into or out of their wetsuits, others maintain all-around defense.

OPERATION LOW PROFILE

Once the land operation is complete, you return to the beach and change back into your wetsuits for the swim back to the boats. In training, you learn to carry out these transitions as quickly and efficiently as possible, while maintaining a low profile.

EQUIPMENT WATCH

When this kind of operation is carried out at night and in adverse weather conditions, there is a danger of equipment being lost. You are trained to look out for your colleagues and check one other's equipment.

▼ FIND YOUR LAND LEGS

Once they emerge from the sea, combat divers have to perform their mission like land-based operators. This requires special qualities and fitness.

10 INFILTRATION AND EXTRACTION

Success of a Special Forces mission depends upon the element of surprise, on covert movement, and on the units' ability to perform their roles with precision and accuracy.

76 Parachuting

Conventional parachute operations are planned to get a large numbers of troops on the ground as quickly and as safely as possible, well away from the immediate threat area.

STATIC LINE JUMPS

Conventional operations are normally conducted in daylight and mostly involve static line parachute drops. Large numbers of soldiers rig up to an onboard static line system. The line system opens the parachute automatically with the force of the jump.

▼ QUICK ENTRANCE

Static line parachute jumps rely on automatic parachute opening and are normally used in conventional operations where there is no immediate threat over the drop zone.

SPECIAL FORCES AIDES

Infiltration and extraction (delivery to and removal from the mission zone) involves close cooperation with service personnel who are essential to a mission's success. These include the pilots of airplanes and helicopters, and the coxswains of water craft—along with their associated crew. Special Forces depend on these service personnel to position them in the right place at the right time and to get them out again, sometimes under heavy enemy fire.

▲ PREPARE TO JUMP

Soldiers of 2 Commando Regiment, Australian
Defense Force perform a mass jump from an
MC-130 aircraft over the Great Barrier Reef.

FREE-FALL OPERATIONS

Free-fall parachute operations are conducted
in a clandestine way to avoid detection from
the ground. For a free-fall operation you would
use the Ram-Air Parachute System (RAPS).
Designed to be highly maneuverable, it can
carry you forward at up to 30 mph (50 km/h). It
has long-distance flight capability.

CLANDESTINE DROPS

The maneuverability of the RAPS equipment
makes "stand-off" parachute drops possible.

Stand-off drops are ones made at an angle
to the target area. If you're a operative on a
free-fall mission, you jump well away from the
target zone and guide yourself into the drop
zone. The aircraft does not have to fly over the
sensitive target area, minimizing the chances
of detection.

FREE-FALL EQUIPMENT

Your typical equipment for a military free-fall parachute operation includes:

1 An oxygen system
2 A helmet
3 Goggles
4 An automatic rip-cord release
5 A free-fall altimeter
6 Parachute containers (including spare parachute) and harness
7 Reserve static line
8 Equipment bag with lowering line
9 Your personal weapon

▼ **GEAR UP**

Special Forces operators wait to perform a high altitude free-fall jump. They have oxygen masks and also night-vision devices mounted on their helmets.

77 Stabilizing position

To reach your target with all your equipment—including personal weapons and additional unit weapons such as medium machine guns—you need to be adept at body stabilization.

PARACHUTE POSITIONS

1 POISED EXIT POSITION

As you jump forward from the aircraft, arch your back and extend your arms back and to the sides, with your legs apart (shown below).

2 DIVING EXIT POSITION

Jump backward from the aircraft, arch your back and extend your arms forward and to the sides. Bend your knees and bring the heels of your boots toward your back.

3 STABLE FREE-FALL POSITION

Maintain an arched back, holding your head back. Extend your arms, with your elbows bent at 90 degrees. Hold your hands palm downward and slightly cupped. Your legs are apart with knees bent at about 45 degrees.

4 BODY TURN

To turn, first look in the direction of the turn and then rotate your body in the same direction. As you move to the new direction you counter the turn and carry on with the stable free-fall position.

5 GLIDING

This movement allows you to maintain station with your leader or other members of a team. Bring your elbows into your side and keep your forearms at an angle of 90 degrees to your body. Rotate your shoulders up and forward. Straighten your legs at the knees. Control the speed of your glide with your legs. Straighten your legs for maximum speed.

6 ALTIMETER CHECK

An altimeter check tells you at what point you should be opening your parachute. To maintain the stability of your free-fall, make minimal movements with your head and wrist to check the altimeter reading.

▶ FALL IN LINE

A Special Forces operator demonstrates the diving exit position before he turns to join the rest of the unit as they coordinate their movements toward the landing zone.

78 Deploying your parachute

Once you have reached the agreed altitude, open your parachute by manually pulling the rip-cord handle. After the canopy has fully deployed, use toggles to steer the parachute.

RIDE THE WIND

The RAPS is a sophisticated gliding system that requires high levels of training and proficiency to operate effectively (see page 137). You must know the wind direction and speed to control the canopy and reach your destination successfully.

STAY IN TOUCH

While steering your parachute you must maintain contact with the team leader and stay in the correct position relative to the leader.

NAVIGATE BY LANDMARKS

You may need to navigate by keeping watch for reference points on the ground that allow you to calculate range to the target area against the remaining available altitude. This will be affected by wind direction and strength.

▼ PAY ATTENTION IN CLASS
That seems like a good idea. A student receives instruction on parachute deployment during a high altitude jump.

79 High Altitude Low Opening (HALO) jumps

HALO operations minimize the chances of operators being seen by enemy observers or detected by radar.

LOW VISIBILITY

Your visibility following a HALO jump is minimized because you delay deploying the parachute until the last possible moment.

The aircraft delivering you can remain high and relatively safe from enemy action and can also drop you at a stand off, or an angle from the designated target area, which means that the aircraft may not have to enter enemy air space.

HIGH ALTITUDE

As a Special Forces operator you will jump from a height of about 35,000 feet (11,000 m) to 15,000 feet (4,600 m). Due to the high altitude, you will wear an oxygen mask and breathe oxygen intensively before the jump in order to reduce the danger of hypoxia.

◀ UNDERCOVER ENTRY
U.S. soldiers perform a HALO jump, to insert soldiers covertly into a designated target area.

ON LIFE SUPPORT?

Making a drop with British Special Forces, you would use the High Altitude Parachutist Life-Support System (HAPLSS) and wear special clothing to cope with the extreme cold at great heights.

BT80

British Special Forces use the BT80 multi-mission parachute system. This is designed to cope with varying levels of parachutist skill, varying opening and landing speeds, different deployment altitudes, and operational requirements that may require you to carry large amounts of equipment.

80 High Altitude High Opening (HAHO) jumps

HAHO parachute drops are used on missions where the element of surprise is a top priority.

HAHO: PROS AND CONS

PROS

- **Distance** The aircraft can maintain maximum stand-off distance, minimizing the risk of alerting enemy radar systems or alerting the enemy with the sound of an aircraft approaching.

CONS

- **Risk** Parachute canopies are deployed early and are therefore at greater risk of being spotted during the descent by observers on the ground. The danger is minimized if the operation takes place at night.
- **Hard** HAHO operations are more physically demanding as the operator remains in the cold upper air for longer than is the case for HALO operations.

HAHO, PIRATES

In April 2009 U.S. Navy SEALs snipers used stand-off HAHO techniques to parachute silently onto the deck of USS *Bainbridge* during a tense situation where Somali pirates were holding the captain of a ship hostage (see also page 160). The stand-off distance meant that the pirates were not alerted by the noise of the aircraft.

HAHO NAVIGATION

As a HAHO parachutist you need first-rate navigation skills to guide yourself and your team toward the target. Pre-plan reference points before the mission. These are guides toward the target zone.

▶ **KEEP YOUR DISTANCE**
A HAHO jump may be carried out in areas where the maximum distance needs to be maintained between aircraft exit and the landing zone.

JUMPING WITH A PASSENGER

In circumstances where you need to enter an operational area with a guide or technical specialist who is not trained in HALO or HAHO jumping, you can carry the passenger using a tandem parachute system to cope with the extra load.

LARGER PARACHUTE, HEAVY LOAD

The tandem parachute system includes a larger parachute than the one for single parachutists. The British system is either the Military Tandem Vectored Parachute System or the newer BT533 system. Your passenger can also carry a rucksack as well as two weapons and an oxygen system.

▼ **ALONG FOR THE RIDE**

A team may need to take a specialist with them who is not trained in high altitude jumping. In these cases, an operator may take a passenger strapped to his chest.

CONTROLLED AERIAL DELIVERY SYSTEM

Sometimes an operation requires significant loads to be delivered into the mission zone. The loads can be delivered by parachute through HALO or HAHO without a human operator on the rig.

These operations use a device called a controlled aerial delivery system. The British BT80/GQ360 Controlled Aerial Delivery System can carry loads of up to 420 lb (190 kg). It uses RAPS equipment (see page 137), with an electronic airborne guidance unit. The unit can operate automatically or be controlled remotely.

81 Landing

Landing with a ram air parachute involves three phases.

THREE-STAGE LANDING

1 DOWNWIND

Go past and to the side of the target area at an altitude of 1,500–1,000 feet (450–300 m) and about 300 feet (90 m) to the side. Fly beyond the target downwind for about 400 feet (120 m).

2 BASE LEG

Gently turn the parachute 90 degrees and fly across 300 feet (90 m) or so to be in line with the target, applying gentle braking.

When you are about 500 feet (150 m) directly downwind of the target and at an altitude of about 500 feet (150 m), make the final turn toward the target.

3 FINAL APPROACH

Having made your braked turn toward the target, move toward the landing point using braking techniques. At a height of 200 feet (60 m), lower your equipment pack.

FOUL-WEATHER LANDING

If you are making the free-fall parachute drop in bad weather, you will have to make adjustments such as applying brakes through cloud.

NIGHT LANDING

A nighttime free-fall drop is the most demanding of all and requires high levels of training. You can wear night-vision goggles.

▼ AIR CONTROL

The sophisticated nature of the ram air parachute allows the operator to pilot them with extreme accuracy.

82 After the jump

If you are taking part in an airdrop into a target zone your next task—after the jump—is to assemble with your fellow operatives.

ASSEMBLE AND MOVE OFF

Once you reach the drop zone, you need to move quickly to assemble all your forces and hide your parachutes. You check the area carefully to ensure you have left no signs of your landing before moving off.

RENDEZVOUS

You may rendezvous with guides already on the ground or make your way to your objective using navigation equipment.

VITAL STATISTICS

A typical ram air parachute system can support 450 lbs (204 kg) suspended weight and can be deployed at an altitude of 25,000 feet (7,620 m). It can attain forward speeds of about 35 mph (56 km/h).

▶ SHARP EXIT

Once on the ground, a soldier needs to quickly gather his parachute and move away from the drop zone.

83 Fast-rope descent

Where mission planners deem it safe enough to deploy a helicopter into an area but not safe enough to land, Special Forces may use a fast rope to get quickly to the ground. The technique was first used by British forces in the Falklands War.

FAST-ROPE PROS AND CONS
PROS

- **Fast** Because the helicopter does not have to land, it can deliver troops and move out of the area quickly.
- **Straightforward** It does not require any hitching or knots for attachment. If you're using the technique, the only points of contact are your own hands, knees, and feet.

CONS

- **Hazardous** You may slip or fall off the rope.
- **Danger of rope burns** Gloves are essential for fast-roping.
- **Not suitable for heavy equipment** Your movement down the rope can be affected by the weight of your equipment.

NIGHT MISSIONS

At night, there is a danger that you may miss the rope completely and fall to the ground. To avoid this, chem lights can be placed at intervals on the rope so that the operator can see the rope and its angle to the ground.

TWICE AS FAST

To increase speed of deployment, two fast ropes can be lowered from either side of the helicopter.

▲ STAY STILL

The movement of the helicopter can make it difficult for an operative to descend quickly and easily.

84 How to fast-rope

To get safely down from a helicopter using the fast-rope technique follow the steps explained below.

FAST-ROPING TECHNIQUE

1 You may be seated or standing before reaching for the rope. If you are **sitting**, the command you will hear to start the fast-rope procedure is "Feet, hands." If you are **standing**, the command is "Hands."
2 When given the signal to go, turn between 45 and 90 degrees and start to descend.
3 Control your speed with the grip of your feet, knees, and gloved hands.
4 To reduce the pressure on your hands, apply more pressure with your feet and knees.

5 If you need to come to a stop on the rope, slide one foot over the other with the rope between your feet and tighten your hands on the rope.
6 About 5 feet (1.5 m) from the ground, spread your legs and bend your knees to absorb the impact of landing.

▼ RAPID TURNAROUND
Fast-rope techniques enable soldiers to get to the ground and the helicopter to get out of the danger area quickly.

85 Rappelling

Rappelling is a familiar skill for civilian rock climbers, but Special Forces use the techniques in mountainous terrain, on buildings, and from helicopters.

SEAT-HIP RAPPEL

The seat-hip rappel involves a sling-rope seat and a snaplink. It is a fast and efficient means of getting to the ground under control.

To construct a rappel seat:

1 Place the middle of a rope on the hip opposite to your brake hand. Your brake hand is your strong hand, so the right hand if you are right handed.

2 Take the rope around the back and tie a double overhand knot in front (see page 27).

3 Pass the two working ends of the rope between your legs and upward toward your back.

4 Pass the two working ends over the rope and around the waist, then pull tight.

5 Pass the working ends of the ropes over the rope that is tied around your waist at the two points above the center of the two rear seat pockets.

6 Tie the two working ends with a square knot (see page 26) and two overhand knots over the hip opposite your brake hand.

7 To hook up, place the square knot and the two overhand knots through the snaplink. After pulling the slack out toward the anchor point, pass the two ropes through the snaplink a second time.

8 Place your guide hand palm up on the rope between the anchor point and the snaplink.

9 Place your brake hand down around the working end of the rope and in the small of your back.

◀ **CHOOSE THE RIGHT TECHNIQUE**
For this near-vertical descent the soldier uses a classic seat-hip rappel with a friction device to help control the rope.

▶ **JUMP INTO ACTION**
Using the correct equipment you can achieve a smooth and rapid descent down a steep gradient.

86 Body rappel

The body rappel has a more complex and secure rope arrangement than the fast rappel technique, also shown below.

HOW TO BODY RAPPEL

1 Face the anchor point, straddling the rope.
2 Pull the rope from behind you, around your hip, diagonally across your chest, and over your shoulder.
3 Hold the rope in your brake hand. Your brake hand is your strong hand, so the right hand if you are right-handed.
4 Turn slightly sideways, then keep your brake hand down to move. Use your other hand on the rope above you as a guide.
5 The ideal body position is at a distinct angle from the rock and with your legs spread.
6 To slow or stop, turn your whole body toward the rock.
7 At all times, keep your feet in contact with the rock face.

FAST RAPPELLING

This is a fast means of rappelling on moderate pitches (slopes that are not too steep).

1 Place yourself side-on to the anchor point.
2 Place the ropes horizontally across your back. The hand furthest from the anchor is your brake hand.
3 To slow or stop, bring your brake hand in front of your body. This will lock the rope. Turn to face the anchor point.

◀▲ FAST RAPPELLING
On a moderate gradient you can descend quickly with the rope arranged in a simplified harness across your back.

87 Special Purpose Insertion and Extraction (SPIE)

Special Forces use the SPIE system for rapid drop or airlift of patrols in areas where planners deem it unsafe for a helicopter to land. This system can be used on rough terrain and on water (see page 152).

RIDING THE SPIE ROPE

1 You wear a special harness with carabiner hooked up to one of the D-rings located at intervals on the SPIE rope. There is also a safety D-ring that requires a second attachment.

2 You and the rest of the team attach yourself to the SPIE rope.

3 Once all the operators are attached to the rope, a signal is given. The helicopter rises to lift you and your fellow operators.

4 The helicopter moves to a safe area where you can all be safely lowered.

UNDER ATTACK

If your patrol comes under attack, you'll have to fire your personal weapons while on the SPIE rope. Take care to fire from the hip and at an angle that will not endanger other operators on the rope.

SPIE ROPE—NIGHT OPS

On a night operation, you pass signals from the SPIE rope to the helicopter crew using chem lights.

▲ UP AND AWAY

A CH-46 Sea Knight helicopter lifts a team of marines off the ground during SPIE rig training.

88 SPIE—Water lift

On some missions combat swimmers may need to be lifted from the sea after an operation has been completed.

UP AND AWAY

1 Helicopter crew lower the SPIE rope to the sea. It has flotation devices attached at intervals.
2 If you are being airlifted, you swim to and clamber onto the rope.
3 As the helicopter lifts upward, you may be dragged through the water before you are pulled clear.
4 The helicopter will carry you to a ship and lower you onto the deck.

ROLL OVER

You are trained to roll on your back when being pulled through the water on a SPIE rope attached to a helicopter.

▼ SAFE LANDING

Aircrew being lowered to the deck of an aircraft carrier using the SPIE technique.

89 Climbing Jacob's Ladder

In a Jacob's Ladder operation, Special Forces use a simple rope ladder extended downward from a helicopter.

▲ GET A GRIP

The Jacob's ladder method of extracting personnel requires the operator to hold on with both his equipment and the added weight of water-logged clothing.

QUICK AS YOU CAN

These operations are used when speed is of the essence. They are ordered to extract Special Forces from an area where it is unsafe or impossible for the helicopter to land.

TWO AT A TIME

1 The helicopter lowers the ladder to the ground (on land operations) or onto the deck of a vessel in the water.

SEA KNIGHT

In the U.S. armed forces, Jacob's Ladder operations are typically carried out using the Boeing Vertol CH-46E Sea Knight helicopter.

2 Keep count When using the ladder, remember only two operators are allowed on the ladder at any one time.

3 Hold on tight You have no harnesses or other equipment attaching you to the ladder. You must hold on firmly with both your hands and feet.

11 ATTACK SKILLS

One of Special Forces' key—and most difficult—roles lies in counterterrorism operations where the margin for error is extremely small. A hostage-taker has only to pull a trigger or hurl a grenade for innocent civilians to be killed. In those moments of suspense, Special Forces soldiers have to act with calmness and circumspection, but still get the job done.

90 Urban operations

Special Forces often operate in urban terrain. Urban areas require extreme vigilance since they are often densely populated with noncombatants.

KEY DIFFICULTIES IN URBAN TERRAIN

If you are involved with planning an operation in an urban area you have to bear in mind that your enemy has many options for concealing themselves.

Because of the high number of civilians, your scope of action is limited by the need to avoid casualties. You will be operating under restrictive rules of engagement, with short detection, observation, and engagement ranges. Your options will also be limited by restricted movement for vehicles and close aerial support. You will be working under decentralized operations.

CAREFUL PLANNING

In urban operations communications and access can be complex. You need to plan routes in and out of an operational area very carefully.

▼ BE VIGILANT
A Colombian Special Forces sniper maintains watch on a public building prior to a conference. Snipers are trained to notice suspicious movements and to act accordingly.

FIGHTING IN BUILT-UP AREAS

Because of their range of specialist training, Special Forces can provide unique advantages in urban areas. If you are serving in an urban setting you may be ordered to:

- Identify and destroy designated targets
- Seize a key objective
- Capture enemy personnel
- Place sensors to gather information
- Relay first-hand intelligence from the ground—as Special Forces, you have the advantage of being trained to understand and speak local languages. This will help you blend in.

AIR DROP

Due to the complexity of urban terrain, Special Forces troops may be dropped onto a rooftop by AH-6 Little Bird helicopters (see page 115).

▲ QUICK OFF THE MARK

Movement in built-up areas presents special challenges and requires highly coordinated moves and fast reactions.

ARMORED VEHICLES

Your unit may use ballistic and mine-proof vehicles such as the Bushmaster Infantry Mobility Vehicle (IMV, see page 109) or the RG 333 Mine-Resistant Ambush Protected Vehicle (MRAP, see page 104).

SPECIAL FORCES BACK UP

As a Special Forces soldier in an urban operation, you might work in liaison with an elite back-up regiment that will act to isolate the area while the operation is carried out. In the U.S. armed forces, this will likely be the 75th Ranger Regiment.

91 Attacking a building

When a Special Forces unit hits a building, they have to do it in such a way that the terrorists inside barely have time to think or to do any harm to hostages.

PIONEERS: BRITISH SAS

Following the rise in terrorist incidents in the early 1970s, the British Special Air Service (SAS) created a Counter Revolutionary Warfare Wing (CRW). This became the model for counterterrorist operations across the globe.

The unit trained extensively in Close Quarter Battle (CQB) techniques. The expertise gained by the SAS in this area was called upon by other nations when their counterrevolutionary warfare units were required to intervene in significant terrorist incidents.

▼ CLEARING A BUILDING
Buildings may contain a number of hazards, from lurking insurgents to explosive devices and booby traps.

1980 LONDON IRANIAN EMBASSY SIEGE

In May 1980, the British SAS had the chance to demonstrate their skills in a live crisis. Six gunmen fighting for the autonomy of Khuzestan (an Iranian province) took 26 hostages in the Iranian Embassy in London. Due to the danger to the hostages, the operation took place in daylight:

- More than 30 masked troops stormed the building.
- Five gunmen were killed and one arrested.
- Nineteen hostages were freed, one killed and two injured by crossfire. (The other four hostages had been released earlier for medical reasons.)
- The operation was broadcast on live TV.

STUN THE ENEMY

In Special Forces you rely on extreme speed, surprise, and fast reactions. You need to gain an advantage over opponents in the split seconds that it takes to enter a room and identify terrorists. Using stun grenades creates confusion and buys a few extra microseconds.

SAS RAID ON LONDON IRANIAN EMBASSY TECHNIQUES

The Embassy raid demonstrated many textbook aspects of a Special Forces building assault.

1—Meticulous planning and reconnaissance
Began with a personal reconnaissance by the commander of the SAS at the time.

2—Mock-up planning
Based on details of the inside of the building taken from escaped embassy staff.

3—Electronic reconnaissance
Microphones were lowered down chimneys and placed in walls in adjacent buildings.

4—Covert movement
The British police and army liaised with civilian organizations such as gas companies to organize drilling in the street outside to cover noise of any essential preparations.

5—Coordination
The attack was planned to take place at the front and back of the building simultaneously and SAS snipers were on stand-by.

6—Aggression
Even when things did not go to plan, training and determination kept momentum going.

7—Training
The SAS soldiers were trained to the highest standards in skills including explosives (frame charges and stun grenades), precision use of weapons in close quarter battle, rappelling, and communications.

92 Liberating an airliner

Special Forces are also trained to carry out hostage rescues on airplanes and in airports, on trains, and on ships.

In October 1977, Flight LH181, from Palma de Mallorca to Frankfurt (86 passengers and five crew), was hijacked by four members of a Palestinian terrorist group and re-routed to Mogadishu, Somalia. German Grenzschutzgruppe 9 (GSG-9) arrived covertly and successfully assaulted the plane, rescuing the hostages.

FLIGHT LH181 SOMALIA RAID TECHNIQUES

The operation at Mogadishu demonstrated typical Special Forces characteristics.

1 INTENSIVE PLANNING AND REHEARSAL

There were calls for the Special Forces to attack the plane when it was at Dubai but the operators demanded more rehearsal time.

2 COLLABORATION

The operation was carried out alongside carefully planned distractions created by German negotiators and Somali commandos.

3 CAREFULLY SELECTED EQUIPMENT

This included noise-proofed personal equipment and ladders.

4 HIGH SPEED AND ACCURACY

The operators had to identify and shoot the hijackers within a split second of entering the aircraft.

▼ GAIN CONTROL

Airliners present exceptional challenges for Special Forces hostage-rescue
teams. Assaults demand stealth, guile, speed, and hair-trigger responses.

中国南方航空

93 Special Forces snipers

Most Special Forces units include sniper teams.

SNIPER TACTICS

As a Special Forces sniper you are trained to get into position without being seen. This can take hours of work on camouflage and painstaking movement.

1 CAMOUFLAGE

In the field, you are likely to wear a ghillie suit, made of netting and camouflage material designed to break up your natural shape.

2 POSITIONING

Choose a position in which you do not break the skyline or cast a shadow. You must also be aware of whether you are upwind or downwind of your target.

3 MOVEMENT AND TIMING

Once in position, place the rifle in such a way that it can be raised slowly to make a shot, focus on breathing in order to steady the weapon, and squeeze slowly on the trigger.

SNIPER OPERATIONS

As a sniper you are likely to be used in special operations as a back-up to an active attack, to intercept enemy who may be trying to escape, to counter enemy snipers, or as the main focus of the operation.

> ## KEEP YOUR HEAD DOWN
>
> If you are being held by terrorists and Special Forces come to your rescue, do exactly what they tell you and keep your head down. The Special Forces soldiers need a clear line of fire and do not want hostages in the way.

▼ BLEND INTO THE BACKGROUND
A camouflaged sniper aims an L115A3 sniper rifle. Snipers are not only capable of hitting long-range targets but also provide valuable reconnaissance information.

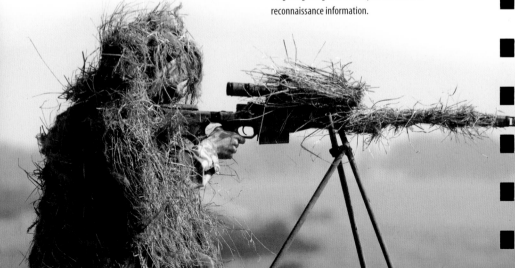

U.S. SNIPERS HIT SOMALI PIRATES 2009

In April 2009, U.S. Navy SEAL snipers parachuted silently on to the U.S.S. *Bainbridge* and took up positions to aim at three Somali pirates who were holding hostage Captain Richard Phillips. One of the pirates held a gun to the captain's head.

The operation was made all the more difficult because both the ship and the pirate's boat were rolling in the waves.

All three pirates had to be hit simultaneously to prevent them killing the captain. The snipers had to judge their moment with extreme precision and coordination, working out the precise time to pull the trigger against the movement of the two vessels. All three shots hit their target and the captain was saved.

▲ A PERFECT VIEW

A sniper is often in a unique position to spot slight enemy movements and to intervene decisively.

SNIPER OPERATION IN BAGHDAD, 2005

In July 2005, snipers of the SAS and the U.S. 1st SFOD-D (Delta) from Task Force Black in Baghdad, Iraq, intercepted suicide bombers about to set out on a mission. All of the suicide bombers had to be hit simultaneously. The British Special Forces used the Accuracy International L115A .338 caliber sniper rifle.

94 Bomb disposal

Special Forces often include bomb-disposal experts. Special Forces soldiers sometimes work with Explosive Ordnance Disposal (EOD) technicians trained to defuse or otherwise neutralize a range of weaponry both in the sea and on land.

BOMB-DISPOSAL MISSION

A typical mission to defuse a land improvised explosive device (IED) is as follows.

1 Clear the area and ensure that it is safe.
2 An electronics expert may provide electronic jamming to prevent the IED from being activated remotely.
3 A bomb-disposal expert will approach the device and lie down near it to minimize the area of their body exposed to any blast.
4 The expert will carefully clear dust and debris from around the device.
5 They will then place a cutting tool next to the wires controlling the device and move

to a safe distance from which he or she can operate the cutting machine remotely.

6 The expert returns to the spot to dismantle the device and arrange for the main charge to be destroyed in a controlled explosion.

▼ A DELICATE OPERATION
A Royal Air Force bomb disposal expert attaches a rocket wrench to a 1,000 lb bomb prior to defusing it.

SPECIAL FORCES BOMB-DISPOSAL TASKS

If you are working as a Special Forces bomb-disposal specialist you will:

- Locate and identify ordnance
- Demolish hazardous munitions, including explosive devices left from previous conflicts, by either detonating or burning them
- Carry out mine-clearance operations at sea to support safe movement of naval vessels
- Use the latest technology, including remote equipment, to make safe unexploded ordnance

▲ DEFUSE THE SITUATION

An Explosive Ordnance Disposal (EOD) specialist spools out detonating cord while preparing to render harmless an unexploded projectile from an anti-tank weapon.

ALL CLEAR?

If you are responsible for clearing the area of a bomb-disposal operation you will need to keep friendly forces out of danger, and be on the lookout for a potential ambush by the enemy. Consider posting snipers to keep watch for enemy movement.

95 Unarmed conflict: knife attacks

The most difficult and dangerous situations a Special Forces soldier will have to cope with is tackling an armed opponent when he or she is weaponless.

TYPES OF KNIFE ATTACK

Knife attacks can be divided into the following categories:

1 **Thrust** Involves jabbing or lunging. It can be extremely dangerous due to the likely damage to your vital organs.
2 **Slash** Normally results from your opponent swinging his or her knife to inflict a cut or gash.
3 **Tear** This type of cut can be made when your opponent slides his or her knife along some part of your body. The wound can be inflicted when your opponent is withdrawing his or her weapon from a thrust.
4 **Hack** Where your opponent's knife is used in a blocking or chopping motion.
5 **Butt** When your opponent uses the handle of his or her knife as a weapon.

DEFENDING AGAINST A KNIFE ATTACK

If your opponent attempts to slash:

1 Strike your opponent's inside forearm with your left forearm.
2 Use your right arm to grab your opponent's knife arm.
3 Turn, holding your opponent's arm close to your body, and use a hold such as a wrist lock or arm bar to take the knife off your opponent.

KEEP YOUR DISTANCE

Defense against a knife attack is complex. Even if you can parry your opponent's thrust, when withdrawing from the thrust your opponent may still inflict a dangerous slash with his or her knife. The basic principle with knife attacks is to remain as far away from the opponent as possible.

◀ LOOK SHARP
Defeating a knife attack is one of the most essential and difficult aspects of personal defense.

▼ HOLD TIGHT

Throwing and disabling the attacker has to be preceded by a firm grip on the knife arm.

96 Defending against hand-to-hand fighting

An unloaded gun is still a major danger if you are being attacked with a rifle with fixed bayonet.

DEFENDING AGAINST A BAYONET STAB

If your opponent attempts to stab you in the stomach with the bayonet, you can:

1 Shift your whole body quickly to the side.

2 Gouge the eyes of your attacker with one hand.

3 Grab the stock of your opponent's weapon with the other hand.

4 Push your opponent away with one hand while disarming him or her with the other.

▼ **PRACTICE MAKES PERFECT**

Marines practice bayonet techniques using sticks. Thorough practice of defense techniques makes survival more likely in real incidents where there is little time to think.

DEFENDING YOURSELF USING A STICK

If Special Forces soldiers do not have a weapon they will use whatever comes to hand—such as a stick—to defend themselves.

BEATING YOUR OPPONENT USING A STICK

The key steps when attacking with a stick are as follows:

1 Grip the stick firmly a few inches from its end.

2 When striking your opponent or your opponent's weapon with a stick, make contact about 2 inches (5 cm) from the top of the stick and with your entire body weight behind it.

3 When striking your opponent, go for maximum effect by hitting bony parts of his or her body such as the wrists, hands, knees, or elsewhere. Other key target areas include the neck, solar plexus, or jugular.

USING A STICK AGAINST A KNIFE ATTACK

A stick can be extremely useful when defending against a knife attack. If your opponent thrusts toward your body, turn aside quickly, and strike hard downward against his or her wrist or arm. Follow up this blow by thrusting your stick into your opponent's throat or adam's apple. Push him or her to the ground with your full body strength.

DEFENDING AGAINST A CHOKE

A choke from behind is a common way for an opponent to try to take control.

1 As soon as you feel your opponent's arm round your neck, grab it with both hands to stop him or her from tightening the choke.

2 Lean forward and, lifting from the hips, throw your opponent over your back.

TYPES OF STICK DEFENSE

There are three main types of defense with a stick:

1 **Thrusting** Grab the stick with both hands and thrust it into the target area with your full body weight behind the thrust.

2 **Whipping** Hold the stick in one hand and make a circular whipping motion.

3 **Snapping** Make short sharp blows with your full body weight behind them.

12 WEAPONS DIRECTORY

Special Forces are familiar with the regular-issue weapons issued to their national armed forces, but are not restricted to these. They often select nonregulation weapons or are equipped with special weaponry specifically developed for their needs. Weapons such as the Combat Assault Rifle (SCAR) are developed specifically for Special Forces and reflect the growing importance of special operations.

L115A3 SNIPER RIFLE

The L115A3 fires the 8.59 mm Lapua round. It has an effective range of 3,600 feet (1,100 m) and is fitted with a five-round magazine. It has a folding bipod and at the end of the barrel there is a suppressor that reduces both flash and noise when the weapon is fired.

SNIPER IMPROVEMENT

The L115A3 was developed as part of the British Army Sniper System Improvement Program (SSIP).

◀▲ L115A3

The L115A3 sniper rifle has a larger caliber and longer range than its predecessor. It has telescopic day/night all-weather sights.

HECKLER & KOCH PSG1 SNIPER RIFLE

This rifle is reportedly used by the U.S. 1st Special Forces Operational Detachment-Delta (1st SFOD-D). It is a semiautomatic sniper rifle with an effective range of 2,600 feet (800 m) firing 7.62 mm NATO cartridges. It can be fitted with a 20-round magazine to make it an effective weapon for rapid fire, and with a flash suppressor and a telescopic sight.

▼ DRAGANOV SVD

This rifle was designed as a squad support weapon for use by marksmen as opposed to highly trained snipers.

MAUSER 86 SNIPER RIFLE

This rifle is a development of the Mauser SP66 sniper rifle and offers greater power and tactical flexibility than its predecessor. It features a manual rotary bolt and a free-floating barrel. It has a rail attachment for a bipod and can take a nine-round magazine. It is fitted with a telescopic sight.

DRAGUNOV SVD SNIPER RIFLE

This rifle is not a standard long-range sniper rifle but was designed to fulfil a role similar to the L129A1 Sharpshooter rifle. It extends your accurate effective range when serving in an infantry unit to about 1,970 feet (600 m). It can be fitted with a PSO-1 optical sight, and can be used in either automatic or single-shot modes.

▼ **DRAGANOV SVD**
U.S. Marines from 1st Platoon, Echo Company, 3rd Assault Amphibian Battalion, 1st Marine Division fire a Dragunov SVD sniper rifle provided by the Mongolian armed forces.

MCMILLAN TAC-50 LONG-RANGE SNIPER RIFLE

The McMillan TAC-50 is a rotary bolt-action rifle with dual front-locking lugs. It can be fitted with a five-round magazine and fires 12.7 mm rounds. To save weight, the rifle has a fluted match-grade barrel and fiberglass stock.

With a McMillan TAC-50 you can fire armor-piercing, incendiary, and explosive rounds—this is a formidable asset against enemy vehicles. If you fire a round into an engine block you can stop a vehicle in its tracks. With a TAC-50 you can also penetrate brick or concrete walls.

BARRETT M82A1 SNIPER RIFLE

This is a longstanding anti-materiel sniper rifle that fires the .50 BMG (12.7x99 mm

LONG RANGE STUNNER

If using the TAC-50 you can comfortably hit long-range targets. A Canadian Forces sniper team of 3rd Battalion Princess Patricia's Light Infantry scored two record-breaking hits with the TAC-50 on deployment in Afghanistan. One shot was at a distance of 7,579 feet (2,310 m) and the other at 7,972 feet (2,430 m). The TAC-50 is the official long-range sniper weapon of the Canadian Forces.

NATO) cartridge. It has an effective range of 5,900 feet (1,800 m). It has a fixed front sight and adjustable rear sight and can also be fitted with optics.

TAKE OUT THE RADAR

In military operations you could use the M82A1 against enemy vehicles, radar installations, or aircraft on a runway.

▼ **BARRETT M82A1 SNIPER RIFLE**

A sniper in training aims a Barrett sniper rifle. On a live operation he would also camouflage the rifle itself.

BATTLE SCAR

The Combat Assault Rifle (SCAR) Modular System was specifically developed for U.S. Special Operations Command and is available in both types of NATO ammunition—5.56 mm and 7.62 mm. The rifles are designated SCAR-L (light) and SCAR-H (heavy).

The rifles include the MK17 long-barrel rifle, designed as an assault rifle with accurate fire at medium to long ranges and the MK20 sniper support rifle. The MK20 is designed to be used by the spotters who often accompany a sniper. If you are a spotter, you need to provide defense for the team. Of course you may also find targets of opportunity while the sniper is otherwise engaged.

An alternative is the MK17 (close-quarter battle), which you would use in short-range operations where accuracy is not at a premium.

The MK17 rifle stock can also be fitted with a MK13 grenade-launcher, which provides the option of both assault rifle fire as well as grenades. The MK13 can also be issued in a stand-alone version.

▼ SCAR
An operator holds the Special Forces Combat Assault Rifle (SCAR). The SCAR system provides a range of options for different missions.

▼ **HECKLER & KOCH G36**

Standard issue for the German Bundeswehr, the G36 is also favored by Special Forces units, including the British SAS.

SAS CHOICE

The G36 is a replacement for the Heckler & Koch G3 SG1 rifle, a weapon of choice for Special Forces units in the past. The G36 is designed for infantry use as well as Special Forces. It is used by the British SAS.

AK-47 TOUGH AND RELIABLE

When using the AK-47 you find its key advantages to be simplicity, robustness, and tolerance of dirt and obstructions that might stop more refined weapons from working. If any weapon merits the term "soldier proof" the AK-47 is it. You can get into all sorts of scrapes with this weapon and it still won't let you down.

HECKLER & KOCH G36 RIFLE

The G36 selective-fire assault rifle can fire rapidly in automatic mode as well as accurately at ranges of 2,600 feet (800 m). It can be fitted with a 30-round magazine of 5.56 mm NATO cartridges.

HECKLER & KOCH 416 ASSAULT RIFLE

The HK 416 is a modular design produced in different barrel lengths for both longer-range and close-quarter battle use. The piston operating system is said to significantly reduce malfunctions.

SG 553

This is an improved version of the SG 552 assault rifle. The rifle fires NATO 5.56 mm ammunition on selective fire with a closed bolt and gas-actuated operating system. The rifle is in service with the Special Forces of France, Germany, and Spain.

AK-47

The AK-47 is the most widely used assault rifle in the world. It is not issued officially to either U.S. or British Special Forces, but as a Special Forces operative you are trained to use and strip down the rifle in case you need to use it on operations abroad. The AK-47 can fire either a 5.56 mm or 7.62 mm cartridge and it has an effective range of 1,300 feet (400 m) in semiautomatic mode.

AK-47 UPDATE

The HK416 assault rifle was developed to fulfil the need for a reliable assault rifle that could cope with extreme operational pressures. The new rifle needed to be more accurate, more reliable, and easy to handle. In other words, it incorporated many of the virtues of the venerable AK-47 in a modern high specification rifle.

COLT M4 ASSAULT RIFLE

The Colt M4 is a 5.56 mm assault rifle designed to fulfil the role of standard infantry weapon for the U.S. armed forces, replacing the M16 rifle. There is a special operations version of the M4 with a variety of add-ons, including sound suppressor equipment, night-vision sight, a laser system, optical scope, and grenade launcher assembly.

▶ **L129A1 SHARPSHOOTER**

British Royal Marines scan for enemy targets. The Sharpshooter bridges the gap between the standard assault rifle and the sniper rifle.

▼ **M4A1 ASSAULT RIFLE**

Special Forces units around the world use a variety of weapons but they all have one thing in common—they need to be reliable when the going gets tough.

▲ **M4A1 ASSAULT RIFLE**
U.S. Spec Ops M4A1 assault rifle with RIS/RAS, grenade launcher, and tactical holographic sight.

L129A1 SHARPSHOOTER RIFLE

The L129A1 is accurate to ranges of 2,600 feet (800 m) and can be fitted with optical, thermal, and night-vision sights. It has a foldable foregrip handle and can be fitted with a bipod. The rifle can also be fired in automatic mode.

LONG RANGE ACCURACY

British forces in Afghanistan found they needed a rifle that could provide accuracy at greater ranges than the standard issue SA80 assault rifle. The L129A1 was the result.

98 Machine guns and submachine guns

HECKLER & KOCH MP5

The MP5 counterterrorist submachine gun is one of the most widely used submachine guns in the world. There are about 100 variants of the gun.

The MP5 is a lightweight, air-cooled, roller-delayed blowback weapon that fires from a closed-bolt position. It can fire about 800 rounds of 9x19 mm parabellum per minute and has an effective range of 650 feet (200 m). It is fed by a magazine with a capacity of up to 32 cartridges.

Different variants of the MP5 come in either fixed-stock or retractable stock versions.

SILENT HIT

The MP5 is in service with both the U.S. and U.K. Special Forces—including the U.S. Navy SEALs and the SAS. A variant of the MP5 in service with the U.S. Navy has a threaded barrel for fitting a stainless-steel sound suppressor. If you are on mission with the U.S. Navy SEALs you could emerge covertly from water and take out an enemy without giving away your position.

M249 MINIMI LIGHT MACHINE GUN

The M249 is a gas-operated air-cooled light machine gun that fires 5.56x45 mm NATO rounds fed from a belt at a rapid rate of 100 rounds per minute to an effective range of 2,600 feet (800 m). It has a hydraulic buffer in the buttstock to maintain accuracy and reduce the effect of recoil on the operator. It has a folding tripod for use in a prone firing position.

This machine gun provides a high rate of fire while also being highly portable. As it fires 5.56 mm ammunition, the ammunition belts are also relatively light. It is in service with U.S. armed forces as the M249 Light Machine Gun (LMG) and with British forces as the Light Machine Gun (LMG). Both are developments of the original Belgian FN Minimi manufactured by FN Herstal.

▲ M249 MINIMI LMG

The highly portable M249 LMG can put down a devastating fire that will make any opponent think twice.

EASY-USE

If you are equipped with the special operations version of the LMG, you will find that it has a shorter barrel, a collapsible buttstock, and no carrying handle. This makes the weapon easier for you to handle and carry, for example on airborne operations. You can quickly change the barrel when necessary.

◀ HECKLER & KOCH MP5

Chilean Special Forces practice a ship assault armed with the highly regarded H&K MP5 submachine gun. Note the torches mounted under the barrels.

BROWNING M2 .50

The Browning M2 heavy machine gun is one of the longest-serving weapons in the U.S. inventory, alongside the Browning M1911 Hi-Power pistol. Both have been in service since the 1920s.

The M2 is a short recoil operated, belt-fed heavy machine gun firing .50 BMG (12.7x99 mm) NATO rounds at an effective range of 5,900 feet (1,800 m). The British version of the Browning M2 is designated the L1A1 12.7 mm heavy machine gun. It has a soft mount to reduce recoil.

JACKAL'S TEETH

The M2 has been fitted to aircraft, maritime, and river craft and to a range of armored fighting vehicles. It was part of the Weapons Mount Installation Kit (WMIK) for British services' Land Rover Defender and can be fitted to the latest Jackal armored vehicles.

▲ BROWNING M2—RIVERINE
A special warfare combatant-craft crewman assigned to Special Boat Team 22 (SBT-22) reloads a M2HB .50 caliber machine gun.

▶ BROWNING M2—HELICOPTER
An aviation warfare systems operator safety checks a Browning M2 .50 caliber machine gun on a SH-60F Seahawk helicopter.

99 Hand guns

BROWNING 1911 HI-POWER

The Browning Hi-Power is a locked-breech semiautomatic, single-action 9 mm recoil-operated pistol. It carries a 13-round magazine with a 9x19 mm parabellum cartridge. It has an effective range of 160 feet (50 m). The Browning Hi-Power is one of the most longlived in-service weapon designs of all time. Based on a design by John Browning, it was until recently the handgun of choice for the British SAS and also the official handgun of the British army. It has since been superseded by the Sig Sauer P226.

▲ **BROWNING 9MM**
The Browning 9 mm pistol was the mainstay of U.S. and British armed forces for many years.

▼ **BROWNING HI-POWER**
A British soldier aims a Browning 9mm pistol on a shooting range in Basra, Iraq.

SIG SAUER P226

The P226 is a mechanically locked recoil-operated pistol that fires a 9x19 mm parabellum cartridge from a magazine with a maximum capacity of 15 rounds.

ADAPTABLE AND HIGHLY VALUED

The standard service weapon of the British armed forces, the Sig Sauer P226 is also used by British Special Forces. Its British military designation is the L117A1. It is also in service with the U.S. armed forces.

WHEN AT SEA

A naval version of the P226 is issued to the U.S. Navy SEALs. It features a phosphate corrosion-resistant finish on internal parts of the weapon and contrast sights.

COVERT WEAPON

The P229 is a more compact version of the P226, with a shorter barrel. It is designed for operations where you might need to conceal your firearm—for instance, if you are on covert operations in urban areas.

▲ SIG SAUER PISTOL

The new kid on the block, the SS P226 combines Swiss accuracy with German efficiency.

HECKLER & KOCH P11

This unusual handgun is designed specifically for underwater use. It fires steel darts of about 3.9 inches (10 cm) from five barrels. Its effective range is 33–50 feet (10–15 m) underwater.

In the U.S. Navy SEALs or the British Special Boat Service you would carry a conventional hand gun—such as the Sig Sauer P226 or P229—alongside a P11. If you encounter an enemy underwater, you could not fire normal pistol rounds, and the P11 would come into its own.

BERETTA 92FS/M9

This pistol is the current service pistol for the U.S. armed forces under the designation M9. A semiautomatic single-action/double-action pistol with an open-slide design to prevent jamming, it also incorporates a safety system that combines the decocking process with positive thumb safety. The pistol has a 15-round staggered magazine holding 9x19 mm Parabellum cartridges. The latest version of the M9, the M9A1, can be fitted with lights, lasers, and other accessories on a rail.

FGM-148 JAVELIN

The Javelin missile system is now widely used by U.S., British, and Australian forces and in the U.K. has largely replaced the MILAN anti-tank system. It is used by Special Forces—for example, by members of U.S. 10th Special Forces Group (see box at left) and the Australian Special Air Service (SASR) in the Iraq war.

The FGM Javelin missile locks on to its target before launch and is designed to attack its target from above. The missile flies to a height of about 500 feet (150 m) before plunging downward. It is fitted with a double warhead to defeat both reactive armor and the base armor underneath. The fire-and-forget system with the Javelin means that the

BATTLE OF DEBECKA RIDGE, IRAQ

The Javelin was used to great effect by members of U.S. 10th Special Forces Group during the Battle of Debecka Ridge in northern Iraq on April 6, 2003. The U.S. 10th Special Forces Group destroyed two Iraqi tanks and eight armored personnel carriers.

▼ FGM-148 JAVELIN

A Javelin missile is launched by New Zealand Defense Force soldiers. Special Forces armed with this weapon are capable of stopping armored vehicles in their tracks.

operator can immediately change position after firing in order to avoid counterfire. The Javelin missile has an effective range of 8,200 feet (2,500 m).

PORTABLE ANTI-STRUCTURES MISSILE

British forces are issued with the Light Anti-Structures Missile (LASM), a variation on the

▲ **M72 LAW**
Light anti-tank weapons such as the M72 LAW provide a single soldier with devastating fire-power.

M72 Lightweight Assault Weapon (LAW) system. Its key advantage is that it is highly portable. The system has an unguided rocket that is aimed at the target before firing. Effective to a range of 1,600 feet (500 m), the rocket is guided by spring-loaded fins that deploy on exit from the firing mechanism. The rocket is designed to first penetrate a structure before exploding.

TAKING ON ARMORED VEHICLES

When you are serving in Special Forces you often find yourself up against enemy armored vehicles. A portable anti-armor system is a key part of your equipment.

TANK STOPPER

The Multi-Purpose Anti-Armor Anti-Personnel Weapon System (MAAWs) is an 84 mm recoilless shoulder-fired portable anti-personnel system that can stop most enemy vehicles in their tracks.

Glossary

Aircraft survivability equipment (ASE) Mostly electronic equipment designed to minimize aircrafts' vulnerability to attack by enemy weapons and other systems.

Altimeter Instrument that determines altitude, normally fitted to an aircraft or worn by skydivers.

Amplitude The angular distance of a celestial object from true east or west points on the horizon at rising or setting.

Avionics The electronic equipment that controls an aircraft.

Azimuth Horizontal angle or direction of a compass bearing.

Chem lights Tubes filled with chemicals that glow in the dark.

Cryptography The art of solving codes or creating them.

Dead reckoning Calculation of position by estimating distance traveled as well as direction.

Defensive-aids suite System to provide protection for air borne platforms, typically including missile warning systems.

Electronic countermeasures Methods of defending an aircraft from attack, such as jamming missile radar.

Encryption Turning a message into a code.

Extraction (exfiltration) Covert withdrawal of personnel from enemy territory.

Fast-rope Rope system used by military and security personnel to get quickly to the ground, to a building, or to a boat deck from a helicopter.

Fast-burst transmissions Method of sending coded messages quickly in order to avoid hostile radio detection.

Geographic coordinate A place on the ground identified on a map by taking an intersection of eastings and northings.

Grid north North as indicated by the grid lines on a map.

Improvised Explosive Devices (IEDs) Explosive devices often created by terrorists or insurgents from a variety of unrelated bits of equipment.

Infiltration Covert insertion of military personnel into hostile territory.

Infrared camera Camera that can take photographs at night.

Jacob's ladder operations Method of picking up naval or military personnel by lowering a rope ladder into the sea.

Joint Direct Attack Munition (JDAM) A bomb equipped with an inertial guidance system.

Micro-synthetic aperture radar Radar system that uses mathematical techniques to build a high-resolution image of a target.

Minigun Externally powered Gatling gun with a high rate of fire.

Multi-spectral targeting system Sophisticated electronic system that contains multiple sensors for reconnaissance and target acquisition.

Nonpermissive environment An area controlled by hostile forces.

Operation Desert Storm Allied, UN-sanctioned military operation beginning in January 1991 in response to invasion of Kuwait by Iraq.

Overhand knot Also known as simple knot or thumb knot, this is the basic stopper knot.

Rappelling Sometimes called abseiling—lowering oneself under control with a rope and friction device.

Rebreather Device used by divers that purifies and recirculates the diver's breath.

Redundant navigator Back-up navigation system used when primary systems are damaged or otherwise failed.

Remote weapons system Weapons system mounted on a vehicle, aircraft, or unmanned vehicle or aircraft that is controlled either from the interior of the vehicle or aircraft or from a base station.

Scuba gear Self-contained underwater breathing apparatus.

Scud NATO code-name for Russian designed R11, R17, or R-300 tactical ballistic missiles.

Soft-skinned vehicles Vehicles that are not fitted with either anti-ballistic or anti-mine armor.

Stand-off drops A parachute drop, normally at high altitude, whereby the plane dropping the parachutist does not enter a denied area, allowing the parachutist to enter the area with their guided ram air parachute system.

Terrain-following radar Aircraft radar system that guides an aircraft over rises and falls in terrain. Particularly useful for operations conducted at low level at night.

True north The surface direction toward the geographic north pole.

Two-speed transfer gear box A four-wheel drive transfer gear box with options for both high and low range.

UTM grid reference Grid reference using the Universal Transverse Mercator coordinate system.

Index

Figures in bold indicate illustrations

Acknowledgments

Marshall Editions would like to thank the following agencies for supplying images for inclusion in this book:

Page 1, 15 U.S. Navy/Mass Communication Specialist 2nd Class Paul D.Williams; page 2-3 U.S. Air Force/Staff Sgt. Joseph L.Swafford Jr.; page 6 U.S. Navy/Mass Communication Specialist 3rd Class Joshua Scott; page 8–9 U.S. Marine Corps/Sgt. Brian Kester; page 9 U.S. Marine Corps/Lance Cpl. J.J.Harper; page 10 U.S. Army/Master Sgt. Donald Sparks; page 11, 129 U.S. Marine Corps/Lance Cpl. Mark Stroud; page 12–13 The Ministry of Defence/© Crown Copyright/LA(Phot) Gaz Faulkner; page 13 Phoric/Shutterstock.com; page 16 left U.S. Army/Spc. Chelsea Russell; page 16 right U.S. Army/Sgt. Thomas Duval; page 17 U.S. Air Force/SRA BRIAN FERGUSON; page 18 SF photo/Shutterstock.com; page 19 U.S. Marine Corps/Cpl. Aaron Hostuler; page 20 left U.S. Army/Spc. Cody Campana; page 20 right mikeledray/Shutterstock.com; page 21 left Andrey Tarantin/Shutterstock. com; page 21 right nialat/Shutterstock.com; page 23 Kerry Sherck/Getty Images; page 24 left Vincent Drolet Lamarre/Shutterstock.com; page 24 right Mike Petrucci; page 25 top Petr & Bara Ruzicka; page 25 berna namoglu/Shutterstock.com; page 27 U.S. Marine Corps/Official USCM photo by Staff Sgt. Danielle M.Bacon; page 28 U.S. Army/Spc. Nathan Goodall; page 29 U.S. Army/Staff Sgt. Amanda Smolinski; page 30–31 Hywit Dimyadi/Shutterstock.com; page 31 The Ministry of Defence/© Crown Copyright/LA(Phot) Dave Hillhouse; page 32 The Ministry of Defence/© Crown Copyright/Ian

Andrews; page 33 The Ministry of Defence/© Crown Copyright/Ian Andrews; page 34 Tyler Olson/Shutterstock.com; page 35 Pichugin Dmitry/Shutterstock.com; page 36 Regimental Combat Team-7, 1st Marine Division Public Affairs Photo by Cpl. Zachary Nola; page 37 U.S. Air Force/Public Domain; page 38 U.S. Marine Corps/Pfc. Franklin Mercado; page 39 Four Oaks/Shutterstock.com; page 40 U.S. Air Force/Senior Airman Evelyn Chavez; page 41 top Bork/Shutterstock.com; page 41 bottom Utekhina Anna/Shutterstock.com; page 42–43 U.S. Marine Corps/Cpl. Jonathan Wright; page 43 Department of Defence/Lance Cpl. Mark W.Stroud; page 44 U.S. Air Force/Senior Airman Eric Harris; page 45 U.S. Marine Corps/Cpl. Kyle N. Runnels; page 46 U.S. Air Force/Airman 1st Class Briana Jones; page 47 The Ministry of Defence/© Crown Copyright/SAC Devine; page 48 U.S. Marine Corps/Lance Cpl. Jeremy T.Ross; page 49 U.S. Navy/Mass Communication Specialist Seaman Thomas J.Holt; page 50-51 Corporal Raymond Vance, Australian Government Department of Defence; page 51 U.S. Air Force/Tsgt Becky Vanshur; page 52, 150 left U.S. Marine Corps/Lance Cpl. Erik Brooks; page 53 MAJ Rick Brietenfeldt, Maryland Army National Guard; page 54 Army National Guard/Spc. Grant Larson; page 55 U.S. Marine Corps/Sgt. Amber Blanchard; page 56 MANUEL PEDRAZA/AFP/Getty Images; page 57 Scott Nelson/Getty Images; page 59 left U.S. Army/Sgt. 1st Class Michael Guillory; page 59 right The Ministry of Defence/© Crown Copyright/Cpl. Mark Webster; page 60 U.S. Army/Staff Sgt. Michael L. Casteel; page 61 U.S. Marine Corps/Lance Cpl. Emmanuel Ramos; page 62–63 Brian A Jackson/Shutterstock.

com; page 63 U.S. Army/Visual Information Specialist Gertrud Zach; page 64 7505811966/Shutterstock.com; page 65 U.S. Navy/Chief Mass Communication Specialist Yan Kennon; page 66 nito; Shutterstock.com; page 67 top Artography/Shutterstock.com; page 67 left Robert Jakatics/Shutterstock.com; page 67 right U.S. Army/Specialist Michelle C.Lawrence; page 68 KKulikov/Shutterstock.com; page 69 U.S. Air Force/Master Sgt. Jeffrey Allen; page 70 U.S. Air Force/Tech. Sgt. Ashley Bell; page 71, 74 U.S. Navy/Seaman Stephen M.Fields; page 72 U.S. Air Force/Airman 1st Class Daniel Hughes; page 73 U.S. Navy/Mass Communication Specialist 1st Class David Hoffman; page 75 top U.S. Navy/Mass Communication Specialist 2nd Class Michael B.Lavender; page 75 stocker1970/Shutterstock.com; page 76 U.S. Air Force/Staff Sgt. Jonathan Snyder; page 77 U.S. Army/Sgt. Brian Kohl; page 78 Andrey Grinyov/Shutterstock.com; page 79 background fotosutra.com/Shutterstock.com; page 80 U.S. Army; page 81 photo by ISAF Public Affairs; page 82 U.S. Army/Sgt. Joseph Bitet; page 83 NASA; page 84–85 Michal Kaco/Shutterstock.com; page 85, 92 Marsan/Shutterstock.com; page 86 Mike VON BERGEN/Shutterstock.com; page 87 MILpictures by Tom Weber/Getty Images; page 88 U.S. Army/Sgt. 1st Class Michael R.Noggle; page 89 U.S. Air Force/Tech. Sgt. Michael R.Holzworth; page 90 dubassy/Shutterstock.com; page 91 The Ministry of Defence/© Crown Copyright/Cpl. Ian Forsyth RLC; page 93 U.S. Army/Spc. Michael Pfaff, 133rd Mobile Public Affairs Detachment; page 94 Eric Gevaert/Shutterstock.com; page 96 Stocktrek Images/Getty Images; page 97

192

Souvoroff/Shutterstock.com; page 99 U.S. Army/Bob McElroy; page 100 Tatiana Belova/Shutterstock.com; page 101 homeros/Shutterstock.com; page 102–103 U.S. Navy/Chief Mass Communication Specialist Michael B. Watkins; page 103, 127, 182 U.S. Navy/Chief Mass Communication Specialist Kathryn Whittenberger; page 104 U.S. Army/Spc. Amber Leach; page 105 U.S. Army/Sgt. Daniel Love, 7th SFG(A) PAO; page 106 U.S. Department of Defence/Sgt. Teddy Wade; page 107 WO2 Giles Penfound/MOD/Getty Images; page 108 U.S. Marine Corps/Cpl. Timothy P.Chesnavage; page 110 SENA VIDANAGAMA/AFP/Getty Images; page 111 Dawid Konopka/ Shutterstock.com; page 112 U.S. Army/Staff Sgt. Bryan Dominique; page 113 U.S. Navy/Journalist 1st Class Jeremy L.Wood; page 114 U.S. Army/Sgt. Eric Glassey; page 115 U.S. Marine Corps/Chief Warrant Officer 2 Keith A.Stevenson; page 116 U.S. Air Force/Tech. Sgt. DeNoris Mickle; page 117 Jonathan Drake/Bloomberg via Getty Images; page 118–119 Ulf Larsen; page 120–121 U.S. Navy; page 121 U.S. Navy/Senior Chief Petty Officer Andrew McKaskie; page 123 U.S. Navy/PH1 Shane T.McCoy; page 124 U.S. Navy/Mass Communication Specialist 2nd Class Christopher Menzie; page 125 Demotix/Press Association Images; page 126 U.S. Navy/Chief Photographer's Mate Andrew McKaskie; page 128 U.S. Navy/Mass Communication Specialist 3rd Class Martin L.Carey; page 130 Senior Chief Photographer's Mate Andrew McKaskie; page 131 U.S. Navy/Mass Communication Specialist 1st Class Jayme Pastoric; page 132–133 U.S. Army/USASOC; page 134–135 U.S. Army/Sgt. Justin P. Morelli; page 135 U.S. Air Force/Staff Sgt. Sara Csurilla; page 136 U.S. Air Force/Staff Sgt. Angelita M.

Lawrence; page 137 U.S. Special Operations Command; page 138 U.S. Army; page 139 U.S. Air Force/Airman 1st Class Matthew J. Bruch; page 140 U.S. Army; page 141 U.S. Air Force/ Staff Sgt. Stephany D.Richards; page142 U.S. Marine Corps/Cpl. Kyle McNally; page 143 U.S Air Force/ Airman 1st Class Trevor Rhynes; page 144 Jeffrey Allen/USAF/Getty Images; page 145 U.S. Army/Master Sgt. Michele Desrochers; page 146 The Ministry of Defence/© Crown Copyright/LA(PHOT) Dave Jenkins; page 147 © Bundeswehr/PIZ Marine; page 148 U.S. Army/1st Sgt Brandon McGuire; page 149 U.S. Marine Corps/Cpl. Christopher O'Quin; page 150 right U.S. Marines/Cpl. Michael Petersheim; page 151 U.S. Marine Corps; page 152 U.S. Navy/ Photographer's Mate 1st Class Jim Hampshire; page 153 U.S. Navy/Mass Communication Specialist 3rd Class Ryan D.McLearnon; page 154–155 U.S. Navy; page 155 The Ministry of Defence/© Crown Copyright/ LA(Phot) Stuart Hill; page 156 MANUEL PEDRAZA/AFP/Getty Images; page 157 U.S. Navy/Mass Communication Specialist 1st Class (AW/SW/NAC) Keith DeVinney; page 158 British Royal Army Sergeant James Elmer; page 160–161 China Photos/Getty Images; page 162 The Ministry of Defence/© Crown Copyright/Cpl. Russ Nolan RLC; page 163 U.S. Navy/Mass Communication Specialist 3rd Class Jeffrey M. Richardson; page 164 The Ministry of Defence/© Crown Copyright/SAC Phil Major RAF; page 165 U.S. Army National Guard/ Sgt. David S.Choi; page 166, 167 U.S. Army Africa/ Edward N.Johnson; page 168 U.S. Marine Corps/Cpl. Gene Allen Ainsworth III; page 170–171 JOEL SAGET/AFP/Getty Images; page 171 U.S. Navy/Mass Communication Specialist 2nd Class Jeff Troutman;

page 172–173 The Ministry of Defence/© Crown Copyright/Andrew Linnett; page 172 The Ministry of Defence/© Crown Copyright/Sgt. Anthony Boocock, RLC; page 173 U.S. Marine Corps/Lance Cpl. Nathan McCord; page 172–173, 181 zimand/ Shutterstock.com; page 174 U.S. Department of Defence; page 175 U.S. Navy; page 176 ©Bundeswehr/ Rott; page 178 top U.S. Army/SSGT SUZANNE DAY; page 178 below Vartanov Anatoly/Shutterstock.com; page 179 The Ministry of Defence/© Crown Copyright/Cpl. Barry Lloyd RLC; page 180 U.S. Air Force/Tech. Sgt. Rick Sforza; page 183 U.S. Navy/ Photographer's Mate Airman Michael D.Blackwell II; page 184 top The Ministry of Defence/© Crown Copyright/LA(Phot) Brian Douglas; page 184 below The Ministry of Defence/© Crown Copyright/Harland Quarrington; page 185 The Ministry of Defence/© Crown Copyright/Sgt. Mike Fletcher RLC; page 186 New Zealand Defence Force; page 187 U.S. Marine Corps/Sgt. Mark Fayloga

Images from the U.K. Ministry of Defence (Defence Imagery), for more information: http://www. nationalarchives.gov.uk/doc/open-government-licence/.

All other images are the copyright of Marshall Editions. While every effort has been made to credit contributors, Marshall Editions would like to apologize should there have been any omissions or errors and would be pleased to make the appropriate correction to future editions of the book.